Edible Economics

Edible Economics

A Hungry Economist Explains the World

HA-JOON CHANG

ALLEN LANE
an imprint of
PENGUIN BOOKS

ALLEN LANE

UK | USA | Canada | Ireland | Australia
India | New Zealand | South Africa .

Penguin Books is part of the Penguin Random House group of companies
whose addresses can be found at global.penguinrandomhouse.com.

First published in Great Britain by Allen Lane 2022
002

Set in 12/14.75pt Dante MT Std
Typeset by Jouve (UK), Milton Keynes
Printed and bound in Great Britain by Clays Ltd, Elcograf S.p.A.

The authorized representative in the EEA is Penguin Random House Ireland,
Morrison Chambers, 32 Nassau Street, Dublin D02 YH68

A CIP catalogue record for this book is available from the British Library

HB ISBN: 978–0–241–53464–9
TPB ISBN: 978–0–241–58565–8

www.greenpenguin.co.uk

To Hee-Jeong, Yuna and Jin-Gyu

Contents

vii

Contents

PART THREE
Doing Better Globally

PART FOUR
Living Together

Contents

Introduction: Garlic

Manul chang-achi (pickled garlic)
(Korean – my mother's recipe)
Heads of garlic, pickled in soy sauce, rice vinegar and sugar

At the dawn of time, humans suffered in chaos and ignorance (so not much has changed, then). Taking pity on them, Hwanoong, a prince of the Heavenly Kingdom, came down to Earth to visit where Korea is today and established the City of God. Within the city he elevated the human race, giving them laws as well as knowledge about agriculture, medicine and the arts.

Hwanoong was one day approached by a bear and a tiger. They had seen what he had done and, noting the way the world worked now, wanted to switch and become human. He promised them that they would each morph into human form if they went into a cave, avoided sunlight and ate only *manul* (garlic) and *ssook** – for a hundred days. The animals decided to follow the instruction and entered a deep cave.

After only a few days, the tiger rebelled. 'This is ridiculous. I can't live on some stinky bulbs and bitter leaves. I'm quitting,' he said – and swept out of the cave. The bear stuck with the diet and, after the one hundred days, became a beautiful woman, Woong-nyeo (literally Bear-Woman). Woong-nyeo later married Hwanoong and had a son, who became the first king of Korea, Dan-Goon.

*

* This is the slightly bitter, herby East Asian wild plant known as 'Korean mugworts' (*Artemisia princeps*).

My nation, Korea, was literally founded on garlic – and it shows. Check out our diet: Korean Fried Chicken* is a veritable festival of garlic: made with batter studded with chopped garlic, often then slathered in sweet, fiery chilli sauce, plus yet more garlic. Some Koreans find the amount of chopped garlic in the marinade for *bul-gogi* (literally meaning 'fire meat') – thinly sliced flame-grilled beef – insufficient. Their solution? Eat it with raw garlic cloves or grilled slices of garlic. A very popular pickle, *manul chang-achi*, consists of heads of garlic, pickled in *ganjang* (soy sauce), rice vinegar and sugar. Garlic leaves and garlic shoots also get pickled the same way. We eat garlic shoots fried, often with fried dried shrimps; or blanched and dressed in sweetish chilli-based dressing. And then there is our national dish, *kimchi* – pickled vegetables – usually made with *baechoo*, the oriental cabbage (known as Napa cabbage in the US and Chinese leaves in the UK), although it could actually be *any* vegetable. If you know a little bit about Korean food, *kimchi* may immediately make you think of chilli powder. But there are in fact a few types of *kimchi* made without it. However, there is no *kimchi* made without garlic.†

Pretty much every Korean soup is made with a stock laced with garlic, whether it be meat-based or fish-based (typically using anchovy but also shrimp, dried mussel or even sea urchin). Most of those small dishes that cover tables at Korean meals (*banchan*, which translates as 'accompaniments to rice') will have (raw, fried, or boiled) garlic irrespective of whether they contain vegetables, meat or fish, and whether raw, blanched, fried, stewed or boiled.

We Koreans don't just eat garlic. We process it. In industrial quantities. We *are* garlic.

South Koreans went through a staggering 7.5kg of garlic per person per year between 2010 and 2017.[1] We hit a high in 2013 of 8.9kg.[2] That's over ten times what the Italians consume (720g in 2013).[3] When it comes to garlic consumption, we Koreans make

---

* Superior to the other KFC, in my view.
† Except in Buddhist temples. Buddhist monks are not allowed to consume or cook with garlic or onion, as well as (of course) any animal product.

the Italians look like 'dabblers'.* The French, 'the' garlic-eaters to the British and the Americans, only manage a paltry 200g per year (in 2017)[4] – not even 3% of that of the Koreans. Amateurs!

OK, we don't ingest the entire 7.5kg. Lots of garlic gets left in the liquid containing the *kimchi*; that liquid is usually thrown away.[†] When you eat *bulgogi* and other marinated meats, tons of chopped garlic will be left floating around in the meat's marinade. But even allowing for all this squandering of garlic, it's a huge – I mean, huge – quantity.

If you have lived all your life among garlic monsters, you don't realize how much garlic you get through. That was me in late July 1986, when, aged twenty-two, I boarded a Korean Air flight to start my graduate studies in the University of Cambridge. I wasn't quite a complete stranger to air travel with, ahem, four flights under my belt, having twice flown to (and back from) Jeju, the semi-tropical volcanic island south of mainland Korea. It wasn't a lot of flight time. The flight between Seoul and Jeju lasts just under forty-five minutes, so my flying experience at that point was not quite three hours. But it wasn't the prospect of flying that made me nervous.

This was my first time ever leaving South Korea. It wasn't poverty that had kept me grounded. My father had worked as a high-ranking civil servant, and my family was comfortable, if not rich, and could have afforded a foreign holiday. However, in those days no South Korean was allowed to travel abroad for leisure purposes – the government simply wouldn't issue passports for the purpose of leisure. It was the time of government-led industrialization in Korea, and the government wanted to use every dollar of

---

* According to James Fenton, the British poet and journalist, when reporting for the *Independent* newspaper on the eve of the 1988 Seoul Olympics.
† Sometimes Koreans consume the liquid too. They often use it to flavor fried rice (*bokkum-bap*: *bokkum* meaning 'fried' and *bap* meaning, no, not the bread, but rice), especially if it is *kimchi bokkum-bap*. They may pour it into an uninteresting soup noodle to perk it up or mix it with rice if there is nothing else around.

export earnings to buy the machines and raw materials needed for economic development. There was no foreign currency to be 'wasted' on 'frivolous' things like foreign holidays.

To make matters worse, travel from Korea to Britain in those days took an unbelievably long time. Today you can fly between Seoul and London in around eleven hours. The Cold War was in full force in 1982, so capitalist planes from South Korea couldn't fly over communist China or the USSR, not to speak of North Korea. First, we flew to Anchorage, Alaska – nine hours. After two hours refuelling (jet oil for the plane, Japanese *udon* noodle soup for me – the first thing I ever tasted outside Korea), we flew for another nine hours to Europe. But not to London. Korean Air didn't then fly to London. So I spent three hours in Charles de Gaulle airport, Paris, before my final flight. Thus it took twenty-four hours to get from Gimpo Airport Seoul to Heathrow Airport London – nineteen hours in the air and five hours in airports. It was a world away.

It wasn't simply the distance that made me feel alien. The language barrier, the racial differences and the cultural prejudices I was prepared for – at least to an extent. Daylight till ten in the evening and (later) winter nights that start at four in the afternoon, I could just about handle. It was difficult to accept that the highest temperature on a summer's day might be 15, 16 degrees (Korean summers are tropical – 33 degrees, 95% humidity, that sort of thing), but accept it I had to. Even the rain could be borne – though I hadn't realized that it could rain quite so often.*

The trauma was the food. Back in Korea, I had been warned (by books, that is – few Koreans had actually been there) that British food was not the best. But I hadn't realized how bad it actually was.

OK, I found a few items in Cambridge I liked – steak and kidney pie, fish and chips, Cornish pasties – but most things were, to put it mildly, terrible. Meat was overcooked and under-seasoned. It was

---

* But not 'so much'. The rainfall in Korea is about the same as that of the UK, at around 1,200–1,300mm per year. Rain in Korea is concentrated in the summer and thus isn't remotely as frequent as that in Britain.

difficult to eat, unless accompanied by gravy, which could be very good but also very bad. English mustard, which I fell in love with, became a vital weapon in my struggle to eat dinners. Vegetables were boiled long beyond the point of death to become textureless, and there was only salt around to make them edible. Some British friends would argue valiantly that their food was under-seasoned (er, tasteless?) because the ingredients were so good that you oughtn't ruin them with fussy things like *sauces*, which those devious French used because they needed to hide bad meat and old vegetables. Any shred of plausibility in that argument quickly vanished when I visited France at the end of my first year in Cambridge and first tasted real French food.

British food culture in the 1980s was – in a word – conservative, deeply so. The British ate nothing unfamiliar. Food considered *foreign* was viewed with near religious scepticism and visceral aversion. Other than completely Anglicized – and generally dire-quality – Chinese, Indian and Italian, you could not get any alternative cuisine, unless you travelled down to Soho or another sophisticated district in London. British food conservatism was for me epitomized by the now-defunct/then-rampant chain Pizzaland. Realizing that pizza could be traumatically 'foreign', the menu lured customers with an option to have their pizza topped with a baked potato.

As with all discussions of foreignness, of course, this attitude gets pretty absurd when you scrutinize it. The UK's beloved Christmas dinner consists of turkey (North America), potatoes (Peru), carrots (Afghanistan) and Brussels sprouts (from, er, Belgium). But never mind that. Brits then simply didn't 'do foreign'.

Of all the 'foreign' ingredients, the national enemy seemed to be garlic. Back in Korea I had already picked up something about the Brits' dislike of the French predilection for garlic. It was rumoured that the Queen disliked garlic so much that no one was allowed to eat it in Buckingham Palace or Windsor Castle while she was in residence. But, until I got there, I had no idea how much stick garlic-eating came in for. For many, it was an act of barbarism, or at least a passive-aggressive assault on those around you. A South-east Asian friend tells the story of her B&B landlady coming into the room she rented with her Indian boyfriend, sniffing, then asking sharply whether anyone had been eating garlic (I guess it's the kind of thing brown people might get up to when left unsupervised). Worth noting that there were no cooking facilities in her room.

I had moved to a place where the Korean essence of life was an affront to civility, perhaps even a threat to the civilization itself. OK, I exaggerate. You *could* buy garlic in supermarkets – though the bulbs looked small and wan. Italian-style dishes in British cook-books included garlic in their recipes – a few slices where I would have thought at least a few cloves were necessary. Even the college cafeteria served certain exotic dishes which claimed to contain garlic – although I couldn't swear they actually did. To escape this culinary hell, I started to cook for myself.

My cooking skills were, however, rather limited at the time. In those days, many Korean mothers wouldn't even let their sons come into the kitchen ('Your willy* will fall off if you enter the kitchen!' was a familiar refrain). The kitchen was the female domain. My mother wasn't that traditional, so I could do a few things in the kitchen, unlike most of my male friends – make good instant *ramen* (surprisingly difficult to make well), put together decent sandwiches, rustle up fried rice with random ingredients found in the fridge and the cupboard, that sort of thing. But that wasn't much of a foundation. Moreover, I didn't have sufficient incentives to cook. I was living alone, and it frankly is no fun cooking for just oneself. Also, when you are in your twenties, you have a good appetite (in Korea we say that 'in your twenties you can digest even stones'), so I was able to wolf it down even if my college canteen threw at me dry, tasteless roast lamb or if I was served – oh, the horror of horrors – over-cooked pasta in a restaurant. As a result, in the first several years of my life in Cambridge – first as a graduate student and then as a

* Or *gochoo* (chilli), reflecting the Korean passion for spicy hot food.

young faculty member – I cooked only occasionally, and my cooking repertoire and skills grew only very slowly.

This created a crisis. My cooking skills weren't advancing, but my *knowledge* of food was expanding fast. Like the cliché: as an academic, perhaps I was better at theory than practice. But the food gap was becoming ridiculous.

The thing was that I had arrived in Britain on the cusp of a culinary revolution. Cracks were appearing on the mighty edifice of British resistance to 'foreign' food, and culinary traditions from outside were starting to trickle in. In the meantime, British cuisine was slowly starting to be upgraded, reinvented and fused with the new influences. Chefs, restaurant reviewers and food critics were becoming celebrities. Cookbooks were becoming as numerous as books on gardening (that peculiar British obsession – which other country airs gardening programmes on TV at peak times in the evening?). Many cookbooks started featuring food histories and cultural commentaries, and not just recipes. With these changes (and my foreign travel), I increasingly encountered cuisines I had known nothing of. I was fascinated. I started trying different foods. I read cookbooks in bookshops and bought quite a few of them. I read avidly the food reviews and features in newspapers. I was starting my own culinary revolution as well.

The truth of the matter is that Korea then was even more of a culinary island than Britain, albeit one with much tastier food. In Korea in that era, aside from Chinese and Japanese places, we had little foreign food other than what was known as 'light Western', essentially 'Japanized' European food. Typical dishes were: *tonkatsu* (schnitzel made with pork, rather than the original Austrian creation with veal); *hahmbahk* (hamburger) steak (a pale imitation of the French *steak haché*, with cheap fillers, like onions and flour, replacing most of the beef); and (very mediocre) spaghetti Bolognese (which was simply called *supageti*). Hamburgers were a rarity, sold as exotic in the cafeterias of upmarket department stores – and weren't very good anyway. The arrival of Burger

King in the mid 1980s was a cultural event. Most people first learned of pizza around then (Pizza Hut arrived in Seoul in 1985). Before coming to Britain and travelling for work or holiday to the continent, I had never tasted real French or Italian food. The few French and Italian restaurants that we had in Korea at the time served highly Americanized versions. Asian food beyond Japanese or Chinese (no Thai, no Vietnamese, no Indian) was just as mysterious, not to speak of dishes from more remote places like Greece, Turkey, Mexico or Lebanon.

The gap between my food theory and practice started narrowing when I began to cook in earnest once I got married in 1993. Hee-Jeong, my wife, moved from Korea to join me in Cambridge. She couldn't believe that I had more than a dozen cookbooks in my home but had never cooked from them. Given the lack of shelf space in my flat, which was only slightly bigger than a large rug, Hee-Jeong reasonably judged that the books needed be binned, unless they were used.

I started cooking with Claudia Roden's classic, *The Food of Italy*. Italian food, especially southern Italian food, has key ingredients (garlic, chilli, anchovy, aubergine, courgette) that Koreans love, so it came naturally. An aubergine pasta bake with tomato sauce and three cheeses (mozzarella, ricotta and parmesan) was the first Roden dish that I learned to cook. It's still (with a few personal tweaks) a family favourite. Antonio Carluccio's books taught me lots about pastas and risottos. Italian is my main arsenal, but I also love to create, in no particular order: French, Chinese, Japanese, Spanish, American, North African and Middle Eastern dishes. And – as proof of the new era we were living in – I learned many great British recipes, especially from Delia Smith, Nigel Slater and Nigella Lawson. I rarely cook Korean dishes, as Hee-Jeong cooks mean Korean food and I cannily avoid competing with her talent.

While I was learning to cook, Britain's culinary revolution was entering a new, and decisive, phase. One could imagine one magical midsummer-night's-dream evening in the mid-1990s, when the

British people finally awoke to realize that their food was actually terrible. Once you acknowledge that your own food sucks, as the Brits then did, you are free to embrace all the cuisines in the world. There is no reason to insist on Indian over Thai or favour Turkish over Mexican. Everything tasty is fine. What a glorious freedom that brings. The British freedom to consider equally all the choices available has led to it developing perhaps one of the most sophisticated food cultures anywhere.

Britain became a great place to eat. London offers everything – cheap yet excellent Turkish doner kebab, eaten at 1 a.m. from a van on the street; eye-wateringly expensive Japanese *kaiseki* dinner; whatever. Flavours span from vibrant, in-your-face Korean levels to understated but heart-warming Polish. You get to choose between the complexity of Peruvian dishes – with Iberian, Asian and Inca roots – and the simple succulence of Argentinian steak. Most supermarkets and food stores sell ingredients for Italian, Mexican, French, Chinese, Caribbean, Jewish, Greek, Indian, Thai, North African, Japanese, Turkish, Polish, and perhaps even Korean, cuisines. If you want a more specialist condiment or ingredient, it can likely be found. This in a country where, in the late 1970s, according to an American friend who was then an exchange student, the only place you could score olive oil in Oxford was a pharmacy (for softening ear wax, if you're wondering).*

It's a global trend of course. With increase in international trade, international migration and international travel, people everywhere have become more curious about and open to foreign foods. Yet Britain is different – perhaps unique – in that, since its moment of honest self-awareness (foodwise), the country has become entirely relaxed about the food it eats. In Italy and France, where strong culinary traditions are entrenched, the locals are defensive and twitchy about change. You can find their great national food, but little else beyond American fast-food joints, cheap Chinese

---

* Checking today (14 January 2022), Tesco website lists 43 varieties of olive oil, Sainsbury's 60, and Waitrose 70.

restaurants and a couple of shops selling falafels or kebabs (those could be very good, but not necessarily) plus maybe a hugely over-priced Japanese restaurant.

While my food universe was expanding at lightning speed, the other universe of mine – economics – was, sadly, being sucked into a black hole. Up to the 1970s, economics was populated by a diverse range of 'schools' containing different visions and research methodologies – Classical, Marxist, Neoclassical, Keynesian, Developmentalist, Austrian, Schumpeterian, Institutionalist and Behaviouralist, to name only the most significant.* Not only did they coexist but they interacted with each other. Sometimes they clashed in a 'death match' – the Austrians vs. the Marxists in the 1920s and the 1930s, or the Keynesians vs. the Neoclassicals in the 1960s and the 1970s. At other times, the interactions were more benign. Through debates and policy experiments tried by different governments around the world, each school was forced to hone their arguments. Different schools borrowed ideas from each other (often without proper acknowledgement). Some economists even tried the fusion of different theories. Economics until the 1970s was, then, rather like the British food scene today: many different cuisines, each

---

* They had (and still have) different visions in the sense that they had different moral values and political positions, while understanding the way the economy works in different ways. No need here to concern yourself with the exact differences between them. I consider the relative merits of each in my last book, *Economics: The User's Guide* (London: Penguin Books, 2014), if you'd like to know more. The critical thing to keep in mind here is that economics is not a science; there are no perfect provable answers. There is no single economic solution or model that works in all situations – choosing the right economic answer depends on the circumstances of the economy and the conditions it faces. It also depends on what you morally or ethically decide is most important for the country's citizens – as we have seen from the stark international differences in the management of the Covid-19 pandemic and its socio-economic consequences. Economics is a study of human activity with all the emotion, ethical stands and imagination that everything human involves.

with different strengths and weaknesses, competing for attention; all of them proud of their traditions but obliged to learn from each other; with lots of deliberate and unintentional fusion happening.

Since the 1980s, economics has become the British food scene before the 1990s. One tradition – Neoclassical economics – has become the only item on the menu. Like all other schools it has its strengths; it also has serious limitations. This ascent of the Neoclassical school is a complex story, which can't be adequately considered here.* Whatever the causes, Neoclassical economics is today so dominant in most countries (Japan and Brazil, and, to a lesser extent, Italy and Turkey are exceptions) that the term, 'economics', has – for many – become synonymous with 'Neoclassical economics'. This intellectual 'monocropping' has narrowed the intellectual gene pool of the subject. Few Neoclassical economists (that is, the vast majority of economists today) even acknowledge the existence, never mind the intellectual merits, of other schools. Those that do assert the other varieties to be inferior. Some ideas, like those of the Marxist school, they will argue, are 'not even economics'. It's claimed that the few useful insights these other schools once possessed – say, for instance, the Schumpeterian school's idea of innovation or the idea of limited human rationality from the

---

* The story would have many ingredients. Academic factors – like the merits and demerits of different schools and the increasing dominance of mathematics as a research tool (which advanced knowledge of particular kinds while suppressing others) – of course have mattered. However, the ascent has also been critically shaped by power politics – both within the economics profession and in the outside world. In terms of professional power politics, the promotion of Neoclassical economics by the so-called Nobel Prize in economics (it is not a real Nobel prize but only a 'prize in memory of Alfred Nobel', given by Riksbank, the Swedish central bank) has played a big role. In terms of power politics beyond the profession, the Neoclassical school's inherent reticence to question the distribution of income, wealth, and power underlying any existing socio-economic order has made it more palatable to the ruling elite. The globalization of education during the post-Second World War era, in which the disproportionate 'soft' cultural power of the US has been the biggest influence, has played a crucial role in spreading Neoclassical economics, which had become dominant in the US first (in the 1960s).

Behaviouralist school – have already been incorporated into the 'mainstream' of economics, that is, Neoclassical economics. They fail to see that these incorporations are mere 'bolt-ons', like the baked potato on a Pizzaland pizza.*

Some readers may legitimately ask: why should I care if a bunch of academics become narrow-minded and engage in intellectual monocropping? My answer might begin by pointing out that economics is not like studying, say, the Norse language or trying to identify Earth-like planets hundreds of light years away. Economics has a direct and massive impact on our lives.

We all know that economic theories affect government policies regarding taxes, welfare spending, interest rates and labour market regulations, which in turn affect our individual economic situations by influencing our jobs, working conditions, wages and the repayment burdens on our mortgage loans or student loans. But economic theories also shape the long-term collective prospects of an economy by influencing policies that determine its abilities to engage in high-productivity industries, to innovate and to develop in an environmentally sustainable way. But beyond even that: economics doesn't just influence economic variables, whether personal or collective. It changes who we are.

The impact on who we are happens in two ways. Economics creates ideas: different economic theories assume different qualities to be at the essence of human nature, so the prevailing economic theory affects what people see as 'human nature'. The dominance of Neoclassical economics, which assumes that human beings are selfish, in the last few decades has normalized self-seeking behaviour. People who act in an altruistic way are derided as 'suckers' or are suspected of having some (selfish) ulterior motives. Were

* Rather than genuine fusions – like Peruvian cuisine, with its Inca, Spanish, Chinese and Japanese influences, or the dishes by the Korean-American chef David Chang (no relation), with American, Korean, Japanese, Chinese and Mexican influences.

Behaviouralist or Institutionalist economic theories dominant, we would believe that human beings have complex motivations, of which self-seeking is only one of many; in these views, different designs of society can bring out different motivations and even shape people's motivations differently. In other words, economics affects what people see as normal, how people view each other and what behaviour people exhibit to fit in.

Economics also influences who we are by affecting the way the economy develops and thus the way we live and work, which in turn shapes us. For example, different economic theories have different views on whether developing countries should promote industrialization through public policy intervention. Different degrees of industrialization, in turn, produce different types of individuals. For example, compared to those who live in agrarian societies, people who live in more industrialized countries tend to be better at time-keeping, as their work – and consequently the rest of their lives – is organized according to the clock. Industrialization also promotes trade union movements by amassing large numbers of workers in factories where they also need to cooperate much more closely with each other than in farms. These movements in turn create centre-left political parties that push for more egalitarian policies, which may be weakened but do not disappear even when factories disappear, as has happened in most rich countries in the last few decades.

We can go further and assert that economics influences the kind of society we have. First, by shaping individuals differently, different economic theories make societies different. Thus, an economic theory that encourages industrialization will lead to a society with more forces pushing for more egalitarian policies, as explained above. For another example, an economic theory that believes humans to be (almost) exclusively driven by self-interest will create a society where cooperation is more difficult. Second, different economic theories have different views on where the boundary of the 'economic sphere' should lie. So, if an economic theory recommends privatization of what many consider to be essential services – like healthcare, education, water, public transport, electricity and housing – it is recommending that the market logic of 'one-dollar-one-vote' should be expanded against the democratic logic of 'one-person-one-vote' (see 'Chilli' and 'Lime'). Finally, different economic theories have different impacts on economic variables, such as inequality (of income or wealth) (see 'Chicken') or economic rights (labour vs. capital, consumer vs. producer) (see 'Okra'). Differences in these variables, in turn, influence how much conflict exists in society: greater income inequality or fewer labour rights generate not just more clashes between the powerful and those under them but also more conflicts amongst the less privileged, as they fight over the dwindling piece of pie available to them.

Understood like this, economics affects us in many more fundamental ways than when it is narrowly defined – as our income, jobs and pensions. That is why I believe it is vital that we all understand at least some of its principles – not just to defend our own interests but, more importantly, to make our society a better place to live for us and for the coming generations.

When I make this point, some respond that the subject is for 'experts' and not ordinary citizens. It is a technical argument, full of jargon, complex equations and statistics, they say. It is not for most of us.

But is this how it is going to be? Are you just going to be 'hanging on in quiet desperation'* while you watch the world around you being churned and moulded according to some economic theory that you don't understand? Tell me. Are you comfortable with the way your society is being designed? Do you find that the ideas and policies of your governments are aligned with what you believe to be most important for us all? Do you see the tax burden being fairly shared by all the world's biggest corporations, as well as ordinary workers? Do you feel everything possible is done to give every child the fairest chance possible for success in their life? Do you feel the

---

* 'The English way', according to Pink Floyd in their song 'Time' from the album *The Dark Side of the Moon*. But I think many non-English people feel this way about their lives these days.

values of our society emphasize community, common responsibilities and shared goals enough? I didn't think so.

Having cajoled you into taking an interest in economics, I cannot abandon you to it. So, with this book, I am trying to make economics more palatable by serving it with stories about food. But be warned. The food stories are mostly *not* about the economics of food – how it is grown, processed, branded, sold, bought and consumed. These aspects are not usually central to the economic stories I have for you. And there are lots of interesting books about them around. My food stories are a bit like the ice cream that some of your mums may have offered to bribe you to eat your greens – except that in this book ice cream comes first, the greens later (what a deal!).

But they are only a bit like that. The food stories in this book are not true bribes in that bribes are things that you offer to people to make them do things that they don't want to. Many mothers in English-speaking countries who offer ice cream to their children for eating their greens are truly bribing their children because they themselves know that the vegetables are not, well, tasty. In contrast, Indian, Korean or Italian mothers have much less (often no) need for such bribery because their vegetables are a lot more exciting than boiled broccoli, spinach or carrot (which George H. W. Bush, the forty-first US President, that intrepid anti-broccoli campaigner, famously called 'orange broccoli'). In these culinary traditions, the vegetables are rewards enough in themselves (though many children still prefer ice cream to vegetables even in those cultures). In the same way, my economic stories are going to be rewards in themselves because I have made them tastier than the usual by making them more varied in kind and more complex in flavour. Neglected issues are brought up, a plurality of economic theories (instead of just one) are used, the political (and even philosophical) implications of economic policies are discussed, realistic alternatives to current economic arrangements – both existing and imagined – are explored.

Introduction: Garlic

I like to share the food that I love with my friends – by cooking for them, by taking them to my favourite restaurants or even by just talking about certain dishes and salivating together. I'd like my readers, my intellectual friends, to share some of the satisfaction I get from digesting, mixing and fusing different economic theories that help me understand how our world is being run and that give me the tools to think about and build a better world.

PART ONE

Overcoming Prejudices

I

Acorn

Dotori mook
(Korean)
Korean acorn jelly with salad leaves, cucumber and
carrot, with spicy soy dressing

Acorn, the nut of an oak tree, is not exactly a choice food. Some Native Americans, especially in California, and some Japanese are known to have eaten it. They ate acorn when they couldn't afford or locate finer sources of carbohydrate – just as poor northern Italians used to bulk up their wheat flour with chestnut flour for pasta.

Koreans eat acorns (*dotori*) – a lot of them – by making a vegetable jelly (*mook*) out of them. I love *dotori mook*, the nutty and slightly bitter undertone of acorn brought out by the salty and sharp taste of *yangnyum ganjang* – a sauce typically made of soy sauce (*ganjang*), sesame oil and seasoning ingredients (*yangnyum*), such as chopped spring onion, chilli powder, and sesame seeds. If you slice in some cucumber and carrot, it makes a nice salad meal.

However much I like *dotori mook*, I'll admit that it's no delicacy. It's the kind of thing that you eat at makeshift food stalls up in the mountains after a hard morning's climbing or in a local tavern on a cheap night out. It is pretty hard to come up with a delicacy based on acorn.

Unless you feed it to *Ibérico* pigs, also known as *pata negra* (black hoof) pigs. The ham made from the legs of these pigs is known as *jamón Ibérico*. The best quality *jamón Ibérico* is made with free-range *pata negra* pigs that only eat acorns in oak forests in the last stages of their lives and is thus called *jamón Ibérico de bellota* (*bellota* means

3

acorn in Spanish).[5] Acorn gives it a deep nutty flavour that's impossible to match. Despite my fondness for *prosciutto di Parma* with sweet melon, I judge *jamón Ibérico* to be the best ham in the world. I hope my Italian friends, unyielding on the topic of food, forgive me for this. The high price it commands suggests that many people – outside Italy, no doubt – agree with me.

Ham is at the heart of Spanish culture – where else could have produced a movie called 'Ham, Ham' (Penelope Cruz's debut film, *Jamón Jamón*, which also features Javier Bardem)? It became important when the Christians established Spain by fighting the Muslims, who had once controlled most of the Iberian Peninsula. One thing that distinguished the Christians from the Muslims was eating pork; thus pork became a symbol of their Christian identity.[6]

The other non-pork eating folk in Spain – the Jews – also suffered terribly under the Christian resurgence. In 1391, many Jews, threatened by angry Christian mobs, were forced to convert to Christianity on threat of death. Converted Jews were made to eat pork in public, as a demonstration that their conversion was genuine. Some *conversos* secretly practised their original religion, not cooking pork and shellfish, or mixing dairy and meat (and continuing many other practices integral to their rituals and festivities).

When the Spanish Inquisition was established in 1478, one of its goals became catching Jewish pseudo-converts (known as *marranos*, which some believe is derived from the Arabic word meaning pig).* One common method was to watch the chimney of a suspect's house on a Saturday. If the residents of the house were still observing the Jewish Sabbath, the house would have no smoke coming out of the chimney – observant Jews would not cook on that day. It is said that the inquisitors also walked around the alleys on Saturdays identifying houses without cooking smells.[7]

---

* The word *bellota* is also derived from the Arab word for the oak tree, *balewt*, once again affirming the Muslim influence on Spanish culture. I thank Reda Cherif for teaching me this.

In January 1492, the *Reconquista* was achieved. Christians expelled the Muslims from the Iberian Peninsula. Later in the year, a royal decree expelled the Jews from the now-Christian domain. Portugal followed Spain's example. Many Jews expelled from Spain and Portugal fled to the Ottoman Empire, then the centre of the Muslim world. The famous Turkish economist Dani Rodrik is a descendant of one of those people – the original family name, he told me, was Rodriguez, a typical Iberian Jewish name.

Today it seems strange that persecuted Jews would flee to a Muslim country, but it was then an obvious choice. Compared to Spain and other Christian countries, the Ottoman Empire was far more tolerant of religious minorities, including the Jews. Sultan Beyazit II is supposed to have welcomed the Jews with open arms, apparently saying that the Catholic monarch's loss was his gain.

In the Ottoman Empire, like all non-Muslims, Jews had to pay higher taxes, but they were allowed to practise their religion freely and given the autonomy to run their communities as they wished. Jews could be found in every role within the Empire – as courtly advisers and diplomats, merchants and manufacturers, porters and masons. Intolerance is not an inevitable manifestation of Islam, contrary to what some people think.

Other negative cultural stereotypes of Islam don't hold up to scrutiny either. Many people see Islam as a militaristic religion, and fundamentalist Muslims have encouraged that view. Hence the common misunderstanding of the term *jihad* – which originally meant striving towards any worthy goal – to mean a religious war against the infidels. While Islam has a streak that allows for a militaristic interpretation, it also emphasizes the importance of learning, epitomized in the words of Muhammad, the Prophet, that 'the ink of the scholar is more sacred than the blood of the martyr'. Indeed, the Renaissance would have been impossible had Muslims not translated many classical Greek and Latin works into Arabic, preserving them so they could be later retranslated into European languages. The Christians in Europe had neglected or actively destroyed pre-Christian Greek and Latin texts, declaring them heathen.

Another stereotype of Islam is as an other-worldly religion uninterested in practical issues, like scientific progress and economic development. However, Islam has often been attuned to cultural values that promote economic development. In the Middle Ages, the Muslim world was far more advanced in mathematics and science (especially centred around Baghdad in the tenth and the eleventh centuries), as well as legal studies, than Europe was. You only need to see how many scientific words have Arabic origins – alcohol, alkali, algebra, algorithm (the essence of Artificial Intelligence!) and so on (*al* being the definite article in Arabic). Commerce was highly developed: Arab merchants traded with Korea in the east and Africa in the west, not to speak of the Mediterranean world. Merchants had high social status, not least because Muhammad, the Prophet, was a merchant himself. Being a merchant's religion, Islam took contract law very seriously. Muslim countries had trained judges several centuries ahead of Christian countries – in most European countries, you didn't even have to be trained in law to be a judge until the nineteenth century.

Islam possesses another significant characteristic that has the potential to make it more suited for economic development than other cultures. Unlike Hinduism in South Asia or Confucianism* in East Asia, Muslim culture does not have a caste system, which restricts people's choice of occupation according to their birth and thereby limits social mobility. The complexity and the rigidity of the Hindu caste system and its negative impacts on social mobility are well known. Although not as elaborate or as strong, the caste system in traditional Confucian societies was no joke either. There was some degree of social mobility in that the sons (but only sons) of farmers could pass the civil service examination and get incorporated into the ruling caste of scholar-bureaucrats. But this

---

* Confucianism is a political and social philosophy (it's not a religion) invented by the Chinese philosopher Kongzi (a version of whose name, Kongfuzi, has been Latinized into Confucius), who died around the time when the Greek philosopher Socrates was born (early fifth century BCE).

rarely happened in practice. The sons of artisans and merchants (who were just above slaves) were not even allowed to sit for the civil service exam. No wonder that in early modern times, even when the traditional caste system had been formally abolished, Confucian countries still had difficulties in convincing talented youngsters to become engineers (seen as over-educated artisans) or businessmen (the modern equivalent of merchants). These occupations became respectable only when economic development took off in the Confucian countries and made them lucrative and powerful.

So there is nothing inherently anti-developmental about Muslim culture. Lots of its elements suit economic advancement – emphasis on learning, tradition of scientific thinking, lack of social hierarchy, valuing of commerce, strong legalism and tolerance. Malaysia and Dubai both illustrate that Islam is compatible with economic progress.

Ignorance and, sometimes, malice, lead us to use negative cultural stereotyping of 'alien' cultures. We pick only those negative features of a culture that unsettle us and attribute whatever socio-economic problems the countries have to their culture. But this leads us to miss the real causes of their problems.

Cultural stereotyping can be 'positive' – exaggerating the good qualities to be found within a society (usually our own) – but still misrepresents reality and prevents us from understanding the real mechanisms at work.

Many people have attributed the East Asian 'economic miracle' to the region's Confucian culture, which supposedly emphasizes hard work, thrift and education. But which culture doesn't? For example, in trying to explain the economic divergence between South Korea and Ghana, two countries that were at similar levels of economic development in the early 1960s (Korea was in fact much poorer then – in 1961, its per capita income was $93, against Ghana's $190), Samuel Huntington, the veteran American political scientist and author of the controversial book *The Clash of Civilizations*, argues: 'Undoubtedly, many factors played a role, but . . . culture had to be a large part of the explanation. South Koreans valued thrift, investment, hard work, education, organisation, and discipline. Ghanaians had different values. In short, cultures count.' Huntington's description of Confucian culture is a perfect example of positive cultural stereotyping – only picking elements that fit your characterization of a culture that you want to portray in positive light.

Confucianism is supposed to encourage hard work. Yet in the past East Asians were typically described as lazy by Western visitors. An Australian engineer who toured factories in Japan in 1915, at the request of the Japanese government, to provide advice on productivity improvement said, 'to see your men at work made me feel that you are a very satisfied easy-going race who reckon time is no object. When I spoke to some managers they informed me that it was impossible to change the habits of national heritage.'[8] In 1912, when she toured Japan and Korea, Beatrice Webb, the English sociologist and social reformer, said that the Japanese had 'objectionable notions of leisure and a quite intolerable personal independence'[9] and described my ancestors as 'twelve millions of dirty, degraded, sullen, lazy and religion-less savages who slouch about in dirty white garments of the most inept kind and who live in filthy mud huts'.[10] That's coming from a founder of Fabian *socialism*. We might imagine what typical rightwing white supremacists of the time said about people in Confucian countries.

As for the famous Confucian zeal for education, the education that was traditionally emphasized was what was needed for the civil service exam – political philosophy and poetry. These are not directly useful for economic development. Practical pursuits other than agriculture, such as making things and trading, were looked down upon. Commentators like Huntington praise the discipline that Confucian culture instils in people (although Beatrice Webb only found ill-discipline in Japan and Korea). But that discipline is bought at the cost of conformism. Other commentators have argued that the pressure for conformity means that East Asians lack originality and entrepreneurship, although this assertion is

becoming increasingly less plausible, given the amount of technological innovation, original movies, addictive drama series and
creative music that the East Asians produce these days.

I could offer more deconstruction of positive stereotyping of
Confucianism of the kind that Huntington represents, but you
get the point. In the same way in which Islam could be typecast
in entirely positive light, Confucianism can be presented in
entirely negative light. Cultures have different and complex facets. The tolerant, rule-based, science-oriented and commercially
minded version of Islam is as real as the other-worldly, intolerant
and militaristic version. There is the hard-working, learning-
oriented, thrifty and disciplined version of Confucianism, but there
is also the version that is ineffectual in imposing the culture of hard
work among its populace, restricts social mobility, looks down upon
commerce and industry and suppresses creativity. What a society
makes out of its cultural raw material is in large part a matter of
choice – and thus policy action.

The right economic and social policies can promote development, equal opportunities and other positive things in any cultural
context.

Japan and Korea lacked a modern industrial workforce with the
habit of time-keeping and industrial discipline. This workforce was
forged by concrete actions – the instillation of time-keeping habits
and discipline in schools, an ideological campaign emphasizing the
need for hard work in a 'patriotic war' to 'rebuild the nation' through
economic development, and having a labour law allowing long
hours and harsh work practices.

People made high investments in education in the Confucian
countries not because Confucius emphasized erudition but because
land reform and other policies introduced after the Second World
War increased social mobility and thus the return to education.
Despite Confucianism having been the official state ideology for
several hundred years and despite having been colonized by another
Confucian country, the literacy rate in South Korea was only 22%

when the Japanese colonizers left in 1945. Around the same time, literacy rates were 53% in Buddhist Thailand (1947), 52% in Christian Philippines (1948) and 38% in predominantly Muslim Malaysia (1947).[11]

During the early days of its economic development drive in the 1960s and the 1970s, Korea found the youngsters to be reluctant to take up professions like science and engineering because of the old Confucian cultural prejudices against practical pursuits. In response, the Korean government deliberately restricted university places and funding in humanities and social sciences departments and allowed the best science and engineering graduates to have vastly shortened (mandatory) military service. Of course, producing more science and engineering graduates would have resulted in an army of highly educated unemployeds unless there were suitable jobs for them, as has happened in many other developing countries. In order to avoid this, the Korean government promoted industrialization through public-policy intervention (also see 'Prawn' and 'Noodle'), thereby creating those well-paying and intellectually fulfilling jobs that these science and engineering graduates could take upon graduation.

Seeing that the Confucian countries have some of the highest household savings ratios in the world – in Korea, for example, it reached 22% of GDP in the early 1990s and in China it reached 39% of GDP in 2010 – people have talked of thrift as a cultural trait of these countries. This is wrong.

In the early 1960s, when South Korea was one of the poorest countries in the world, the country's gross (not just household) savings ratio was below 3% of GDP – in 1960, it was not even 1%. Its people were simply too poor to save anything, Confucian culture or not.

Over the next three decades, Korea's savings, especially household savings, rose dramatically. Not due to some revival of Confucian culture – if anything, Confucian culture, essentially an ideology fit for an agrarian society, was weakening all the time during the period, thanks to industrialization and urbanization. Household savings rose mainly because the country grew so fast that the increase in people's consumption could not keep pace with the increase in their income. On top of that, the government severely restricted mortgage loans and consumer loans, in order to maximize lending to producers. Koreans had to save first before they could buy big-ticket items, like a house, car or refrigerator.

When the country abolished these restrictions in the late 1990s, within a few years its household savings plummeted from the height of 22% of GDP in the early 1990s (the highest in the world then) to one of the lowest in the world (3–5%) in a few years' time span. Now, the country's household savings as a proportion of GDP (average during 2005–14) is a mere 5%, less than half those of supposedly 'spendthrift' Latin American countries like Chile (10.5%) or Mexico (11.4%).[12]

It will be silly to deny that culture affects people's values and behaviour and thereby the way in which a nation's economy is organized and develops. But the way it does defies simplistic stereotyping that is so common; all cultures have multiple facets that are complex and constantly evolving. Most importantly, culture is much less powerful than policies in determining individual economic behaviour and national economic performance, whether they are of acorn-eating Koreans or of Muslims who wouldn't eat acorn-eating pigs.

2

Okra

Creole succotash
(North American; adapted from the Treme *cookbook)*
Creole-style stew with okra, sweetcorn, beans, tomatoes,
spicy sausage and prawns (or crayfish)

I first encountered okra in a South Asian restaurant* a couple of years after my arrival in Britain in 1986. It was in a dish called *bhindi bhaji*, which the menu translated as 'sautéed lady finger' for the benefit of non-South Asian customers. There were some vegetables that I had never tasted before coming to Britain but whose existence I had known about through books and movies – broccoli, beetroot, turnip and suchlike. But I had never even heard of okra.

Apart from not being able to see why the vegetable was called 'lady finger', as it was chopped up, obliterating its shape, I wasn't too convinced by the dish. I found the 'slimy' texture (I learned later that the technical term is 'mucilaginous') a little difficult to handle.

I later had much better specimens of *bhindi bhaji* – less slimy, not overcooked, and better spiced. My opinion of the vegetable was improved even more by a dish of delightful *okura tempura* I had in a restaurant in Japan. I also enjoyed *frango com quiabo*, Brazilian chicken sautéed with okra, during one of my visits there. I grew to like okra, although I cannot say that it became a favourite vegetable.

All this changed when I went to a Southern restaurant in Washington, DC. There I had my first gumbo, the Southern soup / stew whose

* See 'Spices' for an explanation of why I call it 'South Asian' rather than 'Indian', as the common practice goes.

defining ingredient is okra (whose other common name in the US is gumbo or gombo), with deep flavours and gooey texture. Then several years ago I tried my hand at my first (and so far the only) dish made with okra, which is a succotash recipe that I picked up from a Southern cookbook.* I was blown away – not by my cooking skill (I wish) but by the gooeyness that okra gave to the dish. The mucilaginous nature of okra that had made my first encounter with it slightly awkward turned out to be the magic quality that made the dish so smooth, so comforting, so heart-melting.

Okra belongs to an illustrious family of plants (*Malvaceae*), which includes such famous members as cotton, cacao, hibiscus and durian.† It probably originated in North-eastern Africa (today's Ethiopia, Eritrea and Sudan), although there is a strong contending theory that traces its origin to South-east Asia and India.[13] According to the dominant theory, okra was domesticated in North-eastern Africa and spread north (the Mediterranean), east (the Middle East, South Asia, China and Japan), and west (West Africa). Korea, sadly, missed out.

Okra was brought to the US and the rest of the Americas by enslaved Africans, together with crops like watermelon, peanuts, rice, sesame, black-eyed peas and bananas (both the dessert banana, commonly known as 'banana', and the plantain, the so-called cooking banana – see 'Banana').[14] The name is a giveaway. The word 'okra' is a derivation from Igbo, one of the main languages of today's Nigeria. 'Gumbo', another common name for the vegetable (as well as the dish in which it is the crucial ingredient) in the US, comes from the languages of Central and South-eastern Africa.

* Succotash (meaning crushed maize) is originally from Native Americans in the north-east of the US. The recipe I use has made it 'Southern' by using the Cajun/ Creole 'holy trinity' (onion, celery and [bell] pepper) as the base, cajun andouille sausage (which I substitute with cooking chorizo) and, of course, okra.
† The famously stinky fruit prized in South-east Asia, which tasted to me like custard mixed with blue cheese and was strangely moreish.

Enslavement of Africans started on an industrial scale when Europeans occupied the New World. Having nearly wiped out the native population (not only through genocide but also by bringing over new pathogens), they desperately needed replacement workers – at the lowest possible prices. Over 12 million Africans were captured by slave traders. Of these, at least 2 million perished during the process of enslavement – the initial process of capture and captivity in Africa, the atrocious Atlantic crossing (called the Middle Passage) and imprisonment in 'seasoning camps' in the Americas, where the captured Africans were broken into submission before they were sold off.

Without these enslaved Africans and their descendants, the European capitalist countries could not have had access to cheap resources that fed their factories, banks and workers – gold, silver, cotton, sugar, indigo, rubber and what have you. In particular, without these people, the US could not have become the economic superpower that it is today. And this is not a rhetorical statement.

We all know that enslaved Africans in US plantations were whipped and tortured to produce cotton and tobacco. But not many of us know how important these crops were for the US economy. These two products alone accounted for at least 25% and up to 65% of US exports throughout the nineteenth century. At its height in the 1830s, cotton alone accounted for 58% of US exports.[15] Without the export earnings from cotton and tobacco, the US could not have imported the machines and the technologies that they needed for economic development from the then economically superior European countries, especially Britain, which, in return, benefited from having access to a vast amount of cheap cotton that fed its textile mills during the Industrial Revolution.

Enslaved Africans didn't just provide (unpaid) labour. They were also very important sources of capital – and this is something, I must confess, I hadn't known until recently. Examining the legacy of slavery for *The New York Times*, American sociologist Matthew Desmond writes: 'Enslaved people were used as collateral for mortgages centuries before the home mortgage . . . In colonial times, when land was not worth much . . . most lending was based on human property.'[16] Moreover, Desmond tells us that these individual-slave-based mortgages were then lumped together to form tradable bonds, just like modern-day ABSs (asset-backed securities) that are created by lumping thousands of house mortgages, student loans and car loans together.* These bonds were sold on to British and other European financiers, enabling the US to mobilize capital on a global scale and also to develop its financial industry into a global player. Without the slaves, the US would have remained a pre-modern economy with a primitive financial sector for much longer than it did.

Enslaved Africans didn't just build the US economy. They also sparked off the geopolitical realignment that eventually made the US into a continental-sized country, although this was *not* done by the slaves in the US.

In 1791, the enslaved people of St Domingue, today's Haiti, rose against French sugar plantation owners, under the brilliant military leadership of Toussaint Louverture, a former slave himself. Louver-ture was captured by the French in 1802 and shipped to France, where he died in captivity a year later. But, in 1804, the enslaved people of St Domingue finally expelled the French and declared independence, with Jean-Jacques Dessalines, who had succeeded Louverture as the leader, at the helm. Upon its foundation, Haiti abolished slavery, becoming the first country ever to do so in human history.

The Haitian revolution had some immediate impacts on the US economy. When the revolt started, a lot of French sugar plantation owners ran away to what is today the US state of Louisiana. It was then a French territory and also very suitable for growing sugar.

---

* These ABSs have been combined, sliced and diced into notorious CDOs (collateralized debt obligations), which played a key role in the 2008 global financial crisis. For a quick, accessible guide to ABSs, CDOs and the 2008 global financial crisis, see Chang, *Economics: The User's Guide*, ch. 8, 'Trouble at the Fidelity Fiduciary Bank'.

They brought over enslaved people who were skilled in sugar-growing and -processing, as well as better farming and processing technologies, taking Louisiana's sugar industry to another level. Five decades later, Louisiana was producing a quarter of the world's cane-sugar supply.[17]

But the most far-reaching – if totally unintended – impact of the Haitian revolution was the so-called Louisiana Purchase of 1803. The bloody nose that he got from the Haitian revolution made Napoleon, the then ruler of France, decide to disengage from the Americas, especially from the country's North American territorial possession. The territory, then called Louisiane, named after Louis XIV,* covered about one-third of current US territory, spanning roughly from Montana in the north-west and the US state of Louisiana in the south-east. The US had been negotiating with France to buy the port of New Orleans and what is now the US state of Florida for a few years previously, but, when he decided to quit the Americas, Napoleon offered to 'sell'† all of Louisiana to the US.

With the Louisiana Purchase, US territory more or less doubled instantly. Initially, mining was the main activity in the new territory. But, as the century progressed and more and more European settlers moved to start farming, the territory turned into the country's (and the rest of the world's) breadbasket, thanks to the huge tracts of the fertile, flat land that it contained (see 'Rye'). This settlement, however, caused untold misery among Native Americans. They were driven off their ancestral lands. Many of them ended up in 'reservations', where they suffered poverty and marginalization.

---

* But then it could have been any of the previous thirteen Louis, unless you know French history. Annoying, this French habit of naming so many kings with the same name.

† 'Sell' here was a massive overstatement because France didn't 'own' the territory in any real sense, except a few limited areas. Most territories in French Louisiana were still controlled by Native Americans and uncharted for the European invaders, so what Napoleon sold to the US was the right to push out Native Americans without French interference.

Many others perished through armed violence, poverty and disease before they even got there.

The Louisiana Purchase subsequently became the stepping stone for the US to reach the Pacific. Its continuous westward movement was concluded with the purchase of the Oregon Territory* from the British in 1846 and the war with Mexico (1846–8), after which Mexico was forced to sell one-third of its territory at a knockdown price.†

So, without the revolt by the enslaved Haitians, France would not have quit its North American territory. This would have meant that the US would have been a big but not a continental-size country, occupying the eastern third of its territory today. It is not clear whether a country of that size could have become the global super-power that it has become.

Slavery formally ended in the US a couple of decades after the country came to be continental sized. In 1862, at a critical juncture in the American Civil War, Abraham Lincoln declared the emancipation of slaves in the US, which became the law for the whole country once the North won the war in 1865. The British Empire had already ended slavery in 1833, although that hadn't prevented its factories and banks from profiting from slave-produced cotton and bonds created out of slave mortgages from the US. In 1888, slavery ended in Brazil, the other major slave-based economy.

The end of slavery in the major slave-owning economies, how-ever, didn't mean the end of unfree labour. Around 1.5 million Indians, Chinese and even Japanese migrated abroad as indentured labourers to work in place of the freed slaves throughout the nine-teenth and the early twentieth century. Indentured labourers were not slaves. However, they had no freedom to change jobs and had only minimal rights during their contract periods (3–10 years).

---

* Comprising today's Oregon, Washington and Idaho.
† This included today's California, Nevada, Utah and parts of Arizona, Oklahoma, New Mexico, Colorado and Wyoming.

Moreover, many of them worked in conditions similar to what the slaves had faced; many were literally housed in the former slave barracks. Most of the 2 million or so ethnic Japanese in Brazil and Peru, Chinese and Indian communities in various parts of the Caribbean and Latin America and Indian descendants in places like South Africa, Mauritius and Fiji are the results of this large-scale international indenture that continued unfree labour for several decades after the abolition of slavery, until the British Empire abolished indentured labour in 1917.

Free-market enthusiasts have often defended capitalism using the language of freedom. The Americans have prided themselves for possessing a 'free enterprise' system. The title of the most influential book by Milton Friedman, the free-market guru, and his wife Rose Friedman is *Free to Choose*. The leading free-market think-tanks regularly publish indexes of economic freedom – Heritage Foundation's Index of Economic Freedom and Cato Institute's Economic Freedom of the World Index are the most well-known ones.

The freedom that free-market advocates value is, however, a very narrow one. First, it is freedom in the economic sphere – freedom for businesses to produce and sell what they find most profitable, freedom for workers to choose their occupations, freedom for consumers to buy what they want. If other freedoms – political or social freedoms – clash with economic freedom, free-market economists have no hesitation in putting the latter first. This is why Milton Friedman and Friedrich von Hayek openly supported the murderous military dictatorship of General Pinochet in Chile. They saw the free-market policies under Pinochet, implemented by the so-called 'Chicago Boys',* as defending economic freedom against 'socialist' policies of Salvador Allende (they weren't *that* socialist,

* These were free-market economists trained in the University of Chicago, which is famous for its free-market economics and where both Hayek (1950–61) and Friedman (1946–77) taught.

but that is another story), the elected president who was killed in the military coup of 1973.*

Moreover, within their narrow concept of economic freedom, the freedom that the likes of Friedman or the Heritage Foundation value the most is the freedom for property owners (e.g., capitalists, landlords) to use their properties in the most profitable way. Economic freedoms of other people that may clash with proprietors' economic freedom – the freedom of workers to take collective action (like a strike), the freedom that a strong welfare state gives to unemployed workers to be a little choosier about their new jobs – are at best ignored and at worst denounced as counter-productive. Worse, if some people were defined as 'properties', like the enslaved Africans, their unfreedom had to be enforced through violence and even a war, so that their 'owners' could freely exercise their property rights.

Over the last century and a half, capitalism has become more humane only because we have restricted the economic freedom of property owners that free-market advocates of capitalism think should be sacrosanct. Society has introduced institutions that protect political and social freedoms against economic freedom of property owners, should they clash with the latter – democratic constitutions, human rights laws and legal protection of peaceful protests. We have restricted proprietors' economic freedom through numerous laws – banning slavery and indenture, protecting the right of workers to strike, instituting the welfare state (see 'Rye'), restricting the freedom to pollute (see 'Lime') and so on.

In the same way in which it binds ingredients in a dish together in cooking, the story of okra told in this chapter binds the intertwined stories of economic and other freedoms and unfreedoms under capitalism – enslaved Africans and their descendants, Native

---

* So that makes Chile the 'patient zero' of neo-liberalism, which was implemented elsewhere only in the 1980s, with Margaret Thatcher and Ronald Reagan leading the charge (see 'Coca-Cola').

Americans, indentured Asians, European plantation owners who used slaves and indentured labourers, and European settler farmers in North America. The story reveals that the relationship between capitalism and freedom has been a complicated, conflictual and sometimes even contradictory one, unlike in the story of unalloyed freedom, told to us by the advocates of free-market capitalism. Only when we understand the complexity of this relationship better, can we begin to understand what to do in order to make capitalism a more humane system.

3

Coconut

Piña colada
(Puerto Rican)
Rum, coconut milk and pineapple juice

In the first three and a half decades of my life, I had a very limited – and rather negative – view of coconut. Until I came to Britain in 1986, I had never even seen a coconut, South Korea being way too northern to grow it and then being too poor to import 'luxury' items like foreign fruits. The only form of coconut that I had encountered was dessicated, shredded flesh mixed in some biscuits that were sold as exotic treats.

My view of coconut had a radical revision when I had my first *piña colada*, during my first tropical beach holiday in Cancún, Mexico, in the late 1990s. I had always been fond of pineapple juice, but when it was mixed with coconut milk and rum, the result was magical. I think I spent half that holiday getting drunk on *piña colada* and the other half chasing after my toddler daughter around the edges of the beach and the pool.

My esteem for the coconut grew as I encountered a series of savoury dishes that use coconut milk. First came Thai curries – both green and red varieties. Then came *laksa*, the spicy Malaysian-Singaporean noodle soup with coconut milk, and *nasi lemak*, the Malaysian-Indonesian rice cooked in coconut milk and pandan leaves, eaten with delightful accompaniments (typically fried dried anchovies, roasted peanuts, half a boiled egg, and cucumber slices) and *sambal* (a chilli sauce). On my trip to Brazil, I fell in love with *moqueca Baiana*, the version of *moqueca*, the Brazilian fish stew, from the state of Bahia, with chilli and coconut milk. When I came across

South Indian and Sri Lankan dishes that use coconut milk to give rich flavour without tasting as heavy as northern Indian ones (I am not, however, saying that I necessarily prefer the former to the latter), my conversion to the cause of coconut was complete.

A quarter of a century on from my first encounter with coconut milk in *piña colada*, I have also come to enjoy other forms of coconut ingestion. I love coconut water, with its refreshing sweet-salty taste. When I go to salad bars in South-east Asia or South America, I make it sure that I pile my plate with palm hearts[18] (although they may not necessarily be made with hearts of coconut palm – other palms are frequently used). I have even come to appreciate – although not quite love – the shredded coconut flesh used in some of the South Indian dishes, like *sambar* or *thoren*, even though I am still not totally convinced by its use in macaroons and other biscuits (some prejudices die hard).

Coconut isn't just for eating. The immature fruit is a ready source of clean water – long-distance sail ships crossing tropical waters are said to have routinely carried immature coconuts as an emergency water supply. Its oil is popular for cooking. It is known to have been the first vegetable oil used by fish-and-chip shops in Britain,* which were set up by Jewish immigrants in the mid-nineteenth century (another example of how many 'British' things are actually of foreign origin; also see 'Garlic').[19] Coconut oil is an important ingredient in soap and cosmetic products. It was used as a lubricant in factories before petroleum-based lubricants took over and used to supply glycerine for the manufacture of dynamites (also see 'Anchovy'). Coir, the fibre from the husk of the coconut, is used in ropes, brushes, sacks, mats and also as stuffing for mattresses. Coconut is also a source of fuel; its husks and shells are made into charcoal, while coconut oil can be made into biodiesel, as it is in the Philippines.

Coconut being such a versatile and useful thing, it has come to

---

* A popular brand was called Nut Lard.

symbolize the natural bounty of the tropics, at least in the minds of many people who do not live there.

It is no coincidence that Bounty is the name of a chocolate bar, popular in Britain and Canada, with a coconut filling – and a coconut tree, clear blue sea, white sand, and an opened coconut on its wrapper. It may not be one of the most famous chocolate bars in the world, but it is still popular enough to be included in the Celebrations miniature chocolate bar collection, made by Mars, Inc., rubbing shoulders with such chocolate bar luminaries as Mars, Snickers, Twix, Galaxy and Milky Way.

The association of coconut with the tropics is so deeply entrenched that the so-called 'Robinson Crusoe economy' model that many economists use in order to teach their students some basic economic concepts is a single-commodity economy producing and consuming only coconut[20] – even though there is actually not a single mention of coconut in *Robinson Crusoe*.*

If the coconut symbolizes the natural bounty of the tropical zone in many people's minds, it is often used to 'explain' the human poverty frequently found in the zone.

A common assumption in rich countries is that poor countries are poor because their people do not work hard. And given that most, if not all, poor countries are in the tropics, they often attribute the lack of work ethic of the people in poor countries to the easy living that they supposedly get thanks to the bounty of the tropics. In the tropics, it is said, food grows everywhere (bananas, coconuts, mangoes – the usual imagery goes), while the high temperature means that people don't need sturdy shelter or much

---

* In terms of fruits, Robinson Crusoe eats lime, lemon, grape and melon that grow on his island. He grows barley and rice (these grew from the husks that had been in the bag of chicken feed that he had found on his wrecked ship and thrown away, thinking that they were empty), hunts goats, and fishes. But there is zero coconut in his diet.

clothing. As a result, people in tropical countries don't *have to* work hard to survive and consequently become less industrious.

This idea is often expressed – mostly in private, given the offensive nature of the argument – using coconut. The proponents of this 'tropical want of work ethic' thesis venture that those tropical countries are poor because the 'natives' lie beneath a coconut tree and wait for coconuts to fall, rather than trying to actively grow or, better still, make things.

Quite a plausible tale – except that it is entirely false.

To begin with, few sensible residents of the tropical countries will lie beneath a coconut tree, even if they wanted a free coconut. If they did, there is a danger that the falling coconut will crush their skulls (people do get killed by falling coconuts, so much so that there is an urban legend that coconuts kill more people than sharks do, which isn't true). So, even if you are the fictitious 'lazy native', you would not lie beneath a coconut tree – you would wait (lying down, if you prefer, although there is no requirement that you do) somewhere else and occasionally check whether any coconut has fallen under the tree.

More seriously, it is a complete myth that people in poor countries, many of which are in the tropics, lack in terms of work ethic. In fact, they work much harder than their counterparts in rich countries.

To begin with, usually a much higher proportion of the working-age population is working in poor countries than in rich ones. According to the data from the World Bank, in 2019, the labour force participation rate* was 83% in Tanzania, 77% in Vietnam and 67% in Jamaica, compared to 60% in Germany, 61% in the US and 63% in South Korea, the supposed nation of workaholics.[21]

In poor countries, a huge proportion of children work, instead of going to school. UNICEF (United Nations International Children's

---

* The labour force participation rate is the number of persons who are either gainfully employed or are currently not working but actively looking for a job, divided by the total working-age population.

Emergency Fund) estimates that, during the 2010–18 period, on average 29% of children aged five to seventeen in the least developed countries (LDCs)* were working (this does *not* include children doing 'children's work' – household chores, taking care of younger siblings, doing paper rounds, that sort of thing). In Ethiopia, nearly half the children were working (49%), while child labour rate (the proportion of children working) was around 40% in countries like Burkina Faso, Benin, Chad, Cameroon and Sierra Leone.[22]

Moreover, in rich countries, the vast majority of people between eighteen and twenty-four, in their physical prime, are in tertiary education (junior colleges, universities and beyond). The percentage of those who are in tertiary education of the relevant age cohort could be as high as 90% in some rich countries (such as the US, South Korea and Finland) whereas it is less than 10% in forty or so poor countries. This means that, in rich countries, most people are not working until they are well into their early adulthood, many of them learning things that may not directly raise their economic productivity, although I believe these are very valuable things for other reasons – literature, philosophy, anthropology, history and so on.

In poor countries, a lower proportion of people survive into post-retirement age (sixty to sixty-seven, depending on the country) than in rich countries. But insofar as they are still alive, old people in poor countries tend to work much later into their lives than do their rich-country counterparts, as many of them cannot afford to retire. A very high proportion of them work until they are physically decrepit, as self-employed farmers and shopkeepers or as performers of unpaid household work and care work.

Moreover, when they work, people in poor countries work for much longer than those in rich countries. People in poorer, 'hotter' countries like Cambodia, Bangladesh, South Africa and Indonesia work around 60–80% longer than do the Germans, the Danes or the

---

* The least developed countries are, roughly, countries with less than $1,000 income, although the exact definition is a lot more complicated than that.

French, and 25–40% longer than do the Americans or the Japanese (who are, by the way, despite their reputation for being 'worker ants', these days working less than the Americans).[23]

If people in poor countries are actually working much harder than their counterparts in rich countries, their poverty cannot be a matter of their diligence. It is about productivity. These people are working much longer hours for much greater proportions of their lives, compared to those in rich countries, but they produce much less because they are not as productive.

This low productivity is, in turn, not even mainly due to the qualities of individual workers, such as their education level or health. These things matter for some high-end jobs. But for most jobs, workers in poor countries are, as individual workers, as productive as their rich-country counterparts.[24] This point is easy to see if you think about the fact that immigrants from poor economies into rich ones experience a vast increase in their productivity upon arrival, despite the fact that they do not acquire extra skills or experience dramatic improvements in health in the process of migration. They experience steep increases in productivity because they are suddenly working with better technologies in better-managed production units (e.g., factories, offices, shops and farms), supported by higher-quality infrastructure (e.g., electricity, transport, internet) and better-functioning social arrangements (e.g., economic policies, the legal system). It is as if a jockey who used to struggle with an undernourished donkey is suddenly riding a thoroughbred racehorse. The jockey's skill matters, of course, but who wins the race is largely determined by the horse – or the donkey – that he is riding.

Now, why poor countries have less productive technological and social arrangements that result in low productivity is a complex story that requires discussion of a whole host of factors that I cannot do justice to in this short chapter: the history of colonial domination that forced countries into specializing in low-value primary commodities (see 'Anchovy'), intractable political divisions, the deficient nature of their elites (unproductive landlords, undynamic capitalist class, vision-less and corrupt political leaders), the unfair nature of the international economic system that favours rich countries (see 'Beef') are only the most important of them.

However, what is clear is that poor people in poor countries are poor largely because of historical, political and technological forces that are beyond their control, rather than because of their individual shortcomings, least of all their unwillingness to work hard.

The fundamental misunderstanding of the cause of poverty in poor countries, represented by the false imagery built around the coconut, has helped the global elites, both from the rich countries and the poor ones themselves, blame the poor individuals in poor countries for their poverty. Perhaps getting the story about the coconut right will help the rest of us force those elites to answer difficult questions about historical injustice and restitution, international power asymmetry and national economic and political reforms.

PART TWO
Becoming More Productive

4

Anchovy

Anchovy and egg toast
(my recipe)
Toast topped with mayonnaise, scrambled egg,
cured anchovy fillets and sprinkled with chilli powder

Anchovy is the proverbial small fish. In Korea, scrawny kids get called 'dried anchovies'. Yet, it is actually the biggest fish in the world – in terms of impact on food cultures. What other fish is eaten in large quantities by the Koreans, Japanese, Malays, Vietnamese, Thais, Indians, French, Spaniards and Italians – and in so many ways?

Outside Asia and the Mediterranean, most people probably encounter anchovies as a pizza topping. These anchovies are the ones filleted, salted, matured and preserved in oil in the Mediterranean style. In southern Italy these cured anchovies are used in pasta sauces. In Piedmont in northern Italy they are made into a garlicky dip called *bagna cauda*, to eat with vegetables, raw or cooked. In the Provence region of France people add capers and black olives to cured anchovies and mash them up to make *tapenade*, as a dip for *crudités* (raw vegetables) or to spread over toasted breads (hmm . . .). In Spain, *boquerones en vinagre*, anchovies marinated in vinegar and oil, is a popular dish in tapas bars. I am salivating as I write.

Go to Asia, and the uses are even more diverse. In Malaysia and Indonesia, anchovies are known as *ikan bilis* and eaten dried and then fried, including as an accompaniment to *nasi lemak*, rice cooked in coconut milk and pandan leaf (see 'Coconut'). Koreans also get through a lot of dried anchovies: they may be eaten as an *anju* (snacks eaten with an alcoholic drink), either on their own or dipped in *gochujang* (Korean chilli *miso*). They also fry dried anchovies, often glazed with soy sauce and sugar, and eat it as a *banchan* (a small dish accompanying rice). Depending on your taste, you might add various nuts and seeds for extra nuttiness or green chillies for extra kick. Many of Korean and Japanese soup-stocks are made with dried anchovies and dried *dashima* (a seaweed more commonly known by its Japanese name, *kombu*, outside Korea) – plus garlic (for us Koreans). In Japan and Korea, anchovies are also eaten raw – as *sashimi* – although it is not a common dish.*

Varied as its use may be, the most important role anchovy plays in many culinary cultures is as the raw material for fermented fish sauce. The Romans are said to have sprinkled their food liberally with *liquamen* or *garum* (there is debate on whether these were essentially the same thing, but it need not detain us here), fermented fish sauces made usually of anchovies, in order to give their dishes *umami* flavour – the deep, savoury flavour that is now recognized as one of the five basic tastes (together with sweet, salty, bitter and sour). Anchovies are the most frequently used fish for Vietnamese *nuoc mam* and Thai *nam pla*. Thai or Vietnamese food is unimaginable without their respective fish sauces. For fish sauce, Koreans are rather loyal to their anchovies, or *myulchi*, with which they make *myulchi-jut*, or fermented anchovy sauce. Good *myulchi-jut* is a key to making good *kimchi*.

Strange it may sound, I believe Americans ought to win the prize for being the biggest fans of fermented anchovy sauce. They drink the stuff (who drinks the stuff? – yuck!). Every Bloody Mary, one of the signature cocktails of the USA (despite being supposedly named after an English queen, Mary, a daughter of Henry VIII and the half-sister of Elizabeth I), contains fermented anchovy sauce, hidden within Worcestershire

---

* This is due to its perishability. Anchovy goes stale very quickly, so it can be consumed in *sashimi* form only very near the places where it is caught.

sauce.* Brits also imbibe it in disguised form when they tuck into their favourite grilled cheese toast ('cheese toastie' – see 'Spices'), splashed with Worcestershire sauce.

Anchovies once delivered a lot of riches as well as rich flavours. They were the root of economic prosperity for Peru in the middle of the nineteenth century. This was *not* because the country exported anchovies.† At the time, Peru had an economic boom based on the export of seabird guano (that is, desiccated bird droppings). It was a highly prized fertilizer, being rich in nitrate and phosphorous and not smelling too offensive. It was also used for the manufacture of gunpowder, as it contained saltpetre, a key ingredient.‡

Peruvian bird guano consisted of the excrement of birds like cormorants and boobies that lived on islands off its Pacific coast. These birds' main diet was fish, mainly anchovies, migrating along the west coast of South America, riding on the nutrient-rich Humboldt current, running from southern Chile to northern Peru. The current is named after Alexander von Humboldt, the Prussian scientist and explorer; in 1802, he set the world record for the then highest climb, by reaching 5,878 metres on the Chimborazo volcano, the highest mountain in Ecuador, at 6,263 metres. He was also one of Peruvian guano's earliest champions in Europe. Guano became so important for Peru that economic historians talk about the 'Guano Era' (1840s–1880s).

Peru wasn't the only country where guano was important. In 1856, the US Congress passed the Guano Islands Act, which allowed US citizens to take possession of islands containing guano deposits

---

* Worcestershire sauce, first commercialized in 1837 by the British company Lea & Perrins (now owned by the US company Kraft Heinz), is made with vinegar, molasses, tamarind, spices, sugar, salt, and fermented anchovies. The exact proportions of these ingredients are, of course, a commercial secret.

† These days, Peru actually does export anchovies directly – made into fishmeal for salmon grown elsewhere, especially in Chile. I thank Andy Robinson for alerting me to this.

‡ Coconut provided the other key ingredient for gunpowder – glycerine. See 'Coconut'.

anywhere in the world, provided that the islands were not occupied or within the jurisdiction of other governments. The Act enabled the US to justify the occupation of over a hundred islands in the Pacific and the Caribbean, countering the British monopoly of the Peruvian guano trade. Britain, France and other countries also occupied islands with guano deposits.

The Peruvian guano boom didn't last long. Thirty years into the boom, the export of Peruvian guano started declining, thanks to over-exploitation. The impact was for a while masked by the discovery in the 1870s of deposits of saltpetre (sodium nitrate), a nitrate-rich mineral that could also be used for fertilizer and gunpowder, as well as a preservative for meat. But Peru's prosperity ended with the War of the Pacific (1879–84), also known as the Saltpetre War, in which Chile occupied all the coastal area of Bolivia (thus rendering the country land-locked) and about half of the southern coastal area of Peru. These areas had huge deposits of saltpetre as well as of bird guano and made Chile very rich.

That didn't last long either. In 1909, the German scientist Fritz Haber invented a method of isolating nitrogen from the air, using high-voltage electricity, to make ammonia, and from it, artificial fertilizer. So, Haber had found a way to make fertilizer literally out of thin air. It won him a Nobel Prize in Chemistry in 1918, but his work in developing poison gases, used in the First World War, earned him such notoriety that the fact that he is a Nobel Laureate is not mentioned in polite company.

Haber's invention was commercialized by another German scientist, Carl Bosch, working for the German chemical company BASF (Badische Anilin und Soda Fabrik, meaning Baden Aniline* and Soda Factory), which bought Haber's technology. Today it's called the Haber–Bosch process. This process made mass-production of artificial fertilizer possible, deposing guano from its throne of the

---

* Aniline, or *Anilin* in German, is a base material for many artificial dyes, including mauve, indigo and yellow colours. It is also used to manufacture various types of medicine.

fertilizer kingdom. Saltpetre, an even more important source of nitrates, lost its value too. Production of naturally extracted nitrates (guano and saltpetre) in Chile crashed from 2.5 million tons in 1925 to just 0.8 million tons in 1934.[25]

Other technological innovations destroyed several primary commodity exporters in the nineteenth century. The invention of artificial dyes in Britain and Germany devastated producers of natural dyes all over the world. Artificial red dyes, such as alizarin, wiped out the riches of Guatemala. At the time, Guatemala heavily depended on the export of *cochinilla* (cochineal), a highly prized crimson dye that was used to dye Catholic cardinals' robes (and used to colour Campari, the Italian liqueur, which features in the popular cocktail Negroni – another fun food fact). Cochineal is derived from *Dactylopius coccus,* the cochineal 'beetle' – which isn't a beetle and doesn't even look like one (it looks more like a woodlouse) . . .

When it developed the technology to produce alizarin out of coal tar in 1868, BASF (which was later mass-producing fertilizer out of thin air) was making the most prized red colour from the blackest thing – coal. BASF also developed the technology to mass-produce artificial indigo, another highly prized dye, in 1897, and destroyed the indigo industry in India, ruining the livelihood of many Indian labourers, not to speak of bankrupting many British and other European indigo plantation owners.

Later, in the 1970s, the Malaysian economy, which was at the time producing half the world's rubber, suffered from the increasing competition from various types of synthetic rubber, developed by German, Russian and American scientists in the first half of the twentieth century. Malaysia subsequently diversified into other primary commodities, like palm oil, and into electronics, but the initial blow from artificial rubber left its economy reeling.

It is not only from the inventors of synthetic substitutes that producers of primary commodities (agricultural and mining products) are threatened. There is also the danger that more efficient producers may emerge quickly because production of primary commodities is relatively easy. Until the 1880s, Brazil had a monopoly over rubber. It made the rubber-producing regions of Brazil so rich that Manaus, the then capital of the rubber economy, had a fabulous opera house (the Amazon Theatre – Teatro Amazonas in Portuguese), where Enrico Caruso, the then brightest rising star of the operatic world, travelled all the way from Italy to sing in 1897. But the Brazilian economy was hard hit when the British smuggled the plants out of Brazil and established rubber plantations in their colonies in Malaysia (Malaya then), Sri Lanka and other tropical areas. In the mid-1980s, Vietnam exported virtually no coffee, but subsequently it increased its coffee export very quickly. Since the early 2000s, it has been the second-biggest exporter of coffee in the world, after Brazil, seriously affecting other coffee-producing countries.*

So, a country's position as a major producer of a primary commodity can easily be undermined because it is, well, easy to produce it. However, there is really no comparison between what Vietnam has done to Brazil, Colombia and other coffee-producing countries, on the one hand, and what the German chemical industry has done to Peru, Chile, Guatemala, India and countless other countries reliant on primary commodities, on the other hand. The ability to develop technologies to manufacture artificial substitutes for

---

* These examples reveal that there is nothing natural about 'natural' resources produced by developing countries. Rubber may be a Brazilian crop, but the three largest producers of rubber these days are Thailand, Indonesia and Malaysia. Brazil isn't even in the top ten. Coffee, which is produced mainly in Latin America and Asia, is an African plant, grown on a scale first in Arabia by the Yemenis. Chocolate is originally from Latin America (Ecuador and Peru), but today the world's top five producers of cocoa are in Africa and Asia (Côte d'Ivoire, Ghana, Indonesia, Nigeria, and Cameroon are the top five producers). Likewise, China was originally the exclusive producer of tea, but these days India, Kenya and Sri Lanka are also major producers of it. All of these products show that what many of us think of as 'natural' endowments are actually the results of colonialism – colonial masters transplanting commercially profitable crops from another part of the world to their colonies and often growing them in slave-based plantations.

natural substances gives an economy the ability to destroy existing markets (say, in bird guano) and create new ones (chemical fertilizers, in this case).

More generally speaking, if you have high technological capabilities, you can overcome the restrictions imposed on you by nature. When the Germans did not have guano deposits, *cochinilla* 'beetles' or indigo plants, they got around the problem by concocting chemical substitutes.

The Netherlands may have very little land (it has one of the highest population densities in the world, outside city- or island-states) but it has become the second-largest agricultural exporter in the world – only behind the USA – because it has found ways to augment land through technologies. The Dutch have multiplied their agricultural landmass through greenhouse farming, which makes it possible to have multiple crops in a year despite the rather cold climate. They have further expanded the landmass thus augmented through hydroponic cultivation, that is, growing plants in shelves of water beds – this has allowed them to stack up multiple layers of plants in the greenhouse on the same landmass. On top of that, they have increased the productivity of the hyper-augmented landmass by supplying the plants with high-quality agrochemicals with maximum efficiency through computer-controlled feeding.

For yet another example, Japan has overcome its lack of natural fuel by coming up with some of the most fuel-efficient technologies in the world. When other technologically less capable countries were hit by the Oil Shocks in the 1970s, they could only cope by reducing oil consumption. Thanks to its technological capabilities, Japan, in contrast, could overcome the problem by making its use of oil more efficient as well as developing a highly efficient nuclear power industry.

History shows that sustainable high living standards can only be acquired through industrialization – that is, the development of the manufacturing sector, which is the main source of innovation and technological capabilities (see 'Chocolate').

When you acquire higher productive capabilities through industrialization, you can overcome the constraints that nature has put on you in the most 'magical' ways – you can conjure up the most vivid red dye from the blackest coal, make fertilizer out of thin air and expand your landmass by many multiples without invading another country. Moreover, when you acquire such capabilities, it becomes possible to sustain your standard of living at a high level over a long period of time, because capabilities do not 'run out' in the way natural resources do, like non-renewable mineral resources, such as saltpetre, or renewable resources that almost inevitably get over-exploited and depleted, like Peruvian guano from birds feeding on anchovies.

5

Prawn – or Shrimp?

Gambas al ajillo
(Spanish)
Prawns and garlic fried in hot oil

I used to think prawn and shrimp were different names for the same thing – the British and the Australians preferring the former and the North Americans the latter. Recently I learned that the two are different species with different body segmentations and gills. Prawns have claws on three pairs of their legs, while shrimps have them only on two pairs.

There is more, but this a book about food and not about biology. What we know is that crustaceans are delicious – fried Mediterranean-style in garlic and oil (say, Spanish *gambas al ajillo*) or barbecued (as in Anglo countries) or wok-fried with sauces Chinese-style, or cooked in delicate spices as in South Asia. The Japanese deep-fry their *ebi* in batter, to make *ebi tempura*, and have it atop *nigiri* sushi – sometimes cooked but also raw. The latter is called *ama ebi*, meaning sweet prawn, as it is, well, sweet (it really is). In Korea, we even make fermented sauce out of them (*saewoo-jut – saewoo* being the Korean word for prawn/shrimp and *jut* being the word for fermented fish sauce, as in *myulchi-jut*, the Korean fermented anchovy sauce). In the northern half of the Korean peninsula (not the same as North Korea), *saewoo-jut* is preferred to *myulchi-jut* as an agent to help *kimchi* ferment more quickly and with deeper flavour. Northerners and southerners, however, would agree that boiled pork should be dipped in nothing else than *saewoo-jut*, when you eat *bossam* – boiled pork wrapped in *baechoo* (oriental cabbage) with *moo namul* (julienne of pickled icicle radish, or *moo*, with chilli powder), *kimchi* and *ssamjang* (Korean *miso* mixed with chopped garlic, sesame oil and honey).

People all over the world love prawn and shrimp so much that huge tracts of mangrove forests are destroyed to make way for prawn/shrimp farms, especially in Thailand, Vietnam and China. According to a 2012 Reuters report, around of one-fifth of the world's mangrove forests had been destroyed since 1980, mostly to make such farms.[26] This is a serious problem, given the valuable environmental benefits the mangroves provide. Among other things, mangrove forests offer protection against floods and storms, serve as nurseries for baby fish (including wild shrimps/prawns themselves) and offer rich sources of food for those who live nearby, both from the water and from the forest.[27]

Thinking about it, this popularity of prawn, shrimp and their relatives is a curious thing.

Reflect on the growing call for eating insects, as a much less environmentally damaging source of protein than meat. Farming insects generates virtually no greenhouse gas and requires only 1.7kg of feed per 1kg of live weight, as opposed to 2.9kg of greenhouse gases and 10kg of feed in the case of beef, the worst offender (also see 'Beef' and 'Lime').[28] Insects also require much less water and land per gram of protein produced compared to animals.[29] Yet, the demand for insects is not taking off, while vegetarianism and veganism are spreading. The spread of insect-eating, especially in Europe and North America, is undermined by the 'yuck factor'. A lot of people find the idea of eating insects disgusting.[30]

But, curiously, most of those who find insect-eating repulsive will happily devour prawns, shrimps and their relatives, such as lobsters and langoustines (crayfish). This is the weirdest of food aversions – at least to me. Crustaceans and insects are both arthropods (creepy-crawlies for you and me) – with tentacles, exoskeletons, segmented bodies and multiple pairs of legs. So why eat the former but not the latter?

Will more people eat insects if we rename them? I think we should call crickets 'bush prawns' and grasshoppers 'field langoustines' (or perhaps 'langoustines des champs' would make them even more popular?).

Some people love eating insects. The Chinese, the Thais and the Mexicans are famous for their entomophagy – a fancy term for insect eating. We Koreans also did until a few decades ago. Fried grasshoppers were quite popular (very similar to Mexican *chapulines*) but by far the most popular was *bun-de-gi*.

Bun-de-gi is the boiled pupa of the silkworm moth, whose scientific name, *Bombyx mori*, has become famous thanks to *Silkworm*, the thriller by J. K. Rowling, writing as Robert Galbraith. In my 1970s childhood, on the way back from school, children would buy a cone (made of rolled-up newspapers) of boiled *bun-de-gi* from street-vendors lining up in areas around schools, vying for children's pocket money with everything you can imagine – lollipops, cotton candy, *popki* (caramelized sugar puffed up by adding baking soda and then flattened into a disc – made world-famous by *Squid Game*), cheap toys and even the male chicks unwanted by the egg industry. I once bought such a chick, but it died pretty soon, breaking my heart. Most of them did.

Silkworm pupa was a popular snack among Korean children in the 1970s because they were tasty (although I personally didn't like them very much) and cheap. They are rich in protein and iron, though schools discouraged children from buying them from street vendors for hygienic reasons. *Bun-de-gi* was cheap because it was a 'waste product' from a large industry – silk manufacturing. Silk was one of Korea's main export items at the time, and, as a result, the silk textile industry produced a lot of unwanted pupae after silk was taken from their cocoons.

Making textiles from silkworms started in China around 2500 BCE, and the Chinese then monopolized it for a couple of millennia. Silk-making then spread to Korea, India and the Byzantine Empire in that order. In Western Europe, a (very) late-comer to the industry, Italy was the most important producer of silk. Some older readers may remember the scene set in a silkworm house in Bernardo

Bertolucci's 1900, a movie about the class conflict in rural Lombardy and the rise of fascism and communism in Italy. In the scene, young Olmo (son of a tenant farmer, whose adult version was played by Gérard Depardieu) and young Alfredo (son of the land-lord, whose adult version was played by Robert De Niro) are talking in a silkworm house, against the background of incessant noise of silkworms munching away at mulberry tree leaves in the shelves, collectively so loud that it sounds like the drumming of heavy rain on the roof.

The biggest silk-producing country in modern times, however, used to be Japan (whose people also apparently ate silkworm pupae). Japan had a long history of silk textile-making, since it got sericulture (that is, growing silkworms) from Korea in the seventh century, but its silk industry came to its own in the early post-Second World War years. In the 1950s, Japan was the world's biggest exporter of silk (both raw silk and silk textile), and silk was the country's biggest export item.

The Japanese were not content with that. They wanted to take on the Americans and the Europeans in steel, shipbuilding, automobiles, chemicals, electronics and other 'advanced' industries. However, their country was technologically backward, so there was no way they could compete in those industries. So the Japanese government protected domestic producers in these industries from foreign competition by imposing high tariffs, that is, import taxes (thus making imports of those goods very expensive), and by banning foreign companies from operating those industries in Japan. It also had to help the national firms in these industries by making the tightly regulated banks channel credits to them instead of engaging in more lucrative activities like mortgage loans, consumer credits or (slightly less lucratively) lending to well-established industries like silk.

There was much criticism of these policies, not just outside but also inside Japan. Critics pointed out that Japan would be better off if it just imported things like steel and automobiles and concentrated on making things like silk and other textile products, which it was good at. If you protect your inefficient producers of, say, passenger cars (like Toyota and Nissan) by imposing tariffs on foreign cars, consumers either have to pay more than the world market price to get better cars from abroad or drive inferior and uglier Japanese cars, they pointed out. Also, by artificially channelling bank loans into inefficient industries, like automobile production, through government directives, they added, you are taking away funds from efficient industries, like silk, that could be using the same amount of capital to produce far more output.

This is an absolutely correct argument – if you take a country's capabilities as a producer as given. However, in the long run, a country can change its productive capabilities and become better at things at which it is not good at today.

This does not happen automatically – it requires investments in better machines, up-skilling workers and technological research – but it can happen. It has happened in Japan – in automobile, steel, electronics and countless other industries. In the 1950s, Japan simply could not compete in the international market in these industries, but by the 1980s, it was a world leader in many. It takes at least two decades to change a country's capabilities to produce in a significant way. This, in turn, means that such change cannot happen under free-trade conditions. Under free trade, the inefficient, immature producers in new industries will quickly get wiped out by superior, bigger foreign competitors.

Protecting immature producers in an economically backward country, in the hope that one day they will become better, is known as the 'infant industry' argument. The term suggests a parallel between economic development and child development. We protect and nurture our children until they grow up and can compete with adults in the labour market. The argument dictates that the government of an economically backward country should protect and nurture its young industries until they develop their capabilities as producers and can compete with superior foreign competitors in the world market.

The theory of infant industry was not created in Japan. It was actually invented in the US – by none other than the country's first finance minister, Alexander Hamilton – that's the face you see on the ten-dollar bill, currently experiencing an unexpected revival through the musical *Hamilton* by Lin-Manuel Miranda. Hamilton argued that the US government should protect 'industries in their infancy' (his words) against superior English and other European competition, as otherwise America would never industrialize.

The plot thickens: Hamilton drew his inspiration from the protectionist policies of Britain in the eighteenth century, especially those under Robert Walpole, when the country started its ascent to global industrial supremacy. Hamilton was often accused of being a 'Walpolean', seeking centralization and meddling in the economy, by his free-trade opponents, like Thomas Jefferson, the first state secretary of the US and its third president (under whom the Louisiana Purchase was made – see 'Okra').[31]

Contrary to their public image today as the homes of free trade, Britain and the US were the most protectionist countries in the world in earlier stages of their economic development. They adopted free trade only after they achieved industrial supremacy (also see 'Beef'). The same goes for most other rich countries. Except for the Netherlands and (until the First World War) Switzerland, all of today's rich countries – from Belgium, Sweden and Germany in the late nineteenth century down to France, Finland, Japan, Korea and Taiwan in the late twentieth century – used infant industry protection for substantial periods of time in order to promote industrialization and economic developments.

All of this is not to say that infant industry protection guarantees economic success. As with children, infant industries can fail to 'mature', if you raise them in the wrong way. In many developing countries in the 1960s and the 1970s, protection was excessive, making the domestic producers complacent; and was not reduced over time, thereby giving no incentive for them to improve productivity. Countries that have most skilfully used infant industry protection, like Japan and Korea, tried to prevent this kind of situation by reducing protection over time, in the same way that parents need to gradually reduce protection and demand more responsibility from children as they grow up.

Without infant industry protection, all those countries that were once economic shrimps – like Britain in the eighteenth century, the US, Germany, and Sweden in the nineteenth century or Japan, Finland and Korea in the twentieth century – would not have been able to turn themselves into the big fish of today's world economy.

6

Noodle

Aubergine Pasta Bake
(Italian; my adaptation from Claudia Roden's
Timballo alle Melanzane)
Penne pasta, aubergine and tomato sauce (tomato, basil and garlic),
topped with three cheeses (mozzarella, ricotta, parmesan) and baked

According to the World Instant Noodle Association (yes, such a body exists), South Koreans are the biggest consumers of instant noodles, going through 79.7 servings per person a year, followed by the Vietnamese (72.2) and, distantly, the Nepalese (53.3).[32] Given that there are just over 51 million of us, this works out to be around 4.1 billion servings of instant noodles per year. That's a lot of noodles.

Most of these are curly, chewy wheat noodles, known as *ra-myun* (or *ramen* in Japanese). Most Korean instant noodles are eaten in soups, made from the soup powder contained in the packet, which ranges from quite spicy to lethally hot, although there are varieties that are served fried or dressed in (usually, although not necessarily, spicy hot) sauces.

And that is just the instant noodle. We have oodles of other noodles.

First, there are plain wheat noodles. There is the soft thin one (*so-myun*), the soft thick one (*kal-gooksoo*)* and the slightly chewy thick one (*garak-gooksoo*, similar to Japanese *udon*). All of them tend to be served in soups that are not spicy (for a change!), but *so-myun* is also

---

* *Kal-gooksoo* literally means 'knife-noodle', as it is made by cutting the dough rather than by extruding the noodle in a machine, as is the case for most other noodles.

served mixed with vegetables (and meat, sometimes) and dressed in various types of sauce (some spicy, some not).

Add extra starch to the wheat noodle and extrude it under high temperature and high pressure, and you get the chewiest noodle in the world – *chol-myun*. This noodle is eaten mixed with fiery, sweet and vinegary chilli sauce and vegetables. The combination of extreme chewiness and tear-inducing chilli sauce makes the experience of eating *chol-myun* the culinary equivalent of a triathlon – extremely difficult but enormously fulfilling.

Mix sodium carbonate (Na_2CO_3) into wheat dough, and you get alkaline noodle, with extra chewiness. This noodle is the most popular type in Korea. *Ra-myun* is an alkaline noodle. And then there is *chajang-myun* (or *jajang-myun*). *Chajang-myun* is a 'Chinese' noodle dish invented in Korea, like the 'Indian' dish chicken tikka masala, invented in the UK. It is made with thick, chewy alkaline noodles and served with a sauce made of pork, onions and other vegetables (potato, courgette, or cabbage, according to your taste), fried in fermented dark soybean paste (*choonjang*). If you are a fan of Korean dramas, you've definitely seen it: it's that noodle with coffee-coloured sauce that people in K-dramas seem to be eating all the time and everywhere – in restaurants, in offices, at home (delivered – few cook it at home) or even in interrogation rooms in police stations.* South Koreans are estimated to go through a staggering 1.5 million servings of *chajang-myun* per day.[33]

Another popular noodle is buckwheat (*mémil*) noodle, of which there are two types. There is the soft one, similar to Japanese *soba*, which is called, very imaginatively, *mémil-gooksoo* (buckwheat noodle). The other, thicker and chewier, type is known as *Pyeongyang naeng-myun gooksoo* (literally meaning 'noodle for Pyeongyang cold noodle'). It has this strange name because it is almost exclusively used for *Pyeongyang naeng-myun*, the cold noodle soup made with beef broth (or pheasant broth, in its original Pyeongyang – the

---

* So *chajang-myeon* is the Korean answer to pizza – a solution for those who want a quick but substantial meal.

North Korean capital – fashion) and seasoned with vinegar and mustard. Sometimes acorn (*dotori*) or arrowroot (*chik*) are added to buckwheat flour, to increase the bulk and to add an earthier flavour.

Koreans also make noodles out of various types of starch, rather than out of flour.* The most eminent in this cateory is *dang-myun*, the glass noodle made of sweet potato starch. The word literally means 'Chinese noodle', with *dang*[†] being the prefix in Korean denoting Chinese origin. The original Chinese version is made with starch from mung beans (or green beans), but we Koreans prefer sweet potato starch (the Chinese use it too). *Dang-myun* is also made with starches from cassava, sweetcorn and potato. The Japanese use potato starch to make their thin glass noodle, called, poetically, *harusame* (spring rain). The most prominent use of *dang-myun* in Korean cooking is in *japchae* (Korean glass noodles fried with julienne of vegetables – see 'Carrot'). It is also used in *mandoo* (filled dumplings), *soondae* (Korean black pudding) and some stews, to bulk things up (as it is cheap and filling) and to give chewy texture to the food.

Curiously, there is no traditional Korean noodle made with rice, despite the fact that rice is the dominant grain in the country – perhaps rice was too precious to 'waste' on noodles. But we are catching up fast. These days South Koreans cannot seem to have enough rice noodles, given the rapidly increasing popularity of *pho*, the Vietnamese rice noodle soup, and *pad Thai*, the fried Thai rice noodle.

In the same way in which we turn all vegetables into *kimchi* (see 'Garlic'), we Koreans turn almost every carbohydrate-rich grain and tuber into *gooksoo* – wheat, buckwheat, sweet potato, potato,

---

* Starch is pure carbohydrate extracted from plant material and processed. Flour is grains ground to a powdery state. These days the word 'flour' is used also to mean all powdery ground-up plant materials, as in 'almond flour' or 'arrowroot flour'.

† The word is derived from *Tang*, the name of the dynasty that ruled China between 618 and 907. Many consider the Tang Empire to be the Golden Age of feudal China.

sweetcorn, cassava, acorn, arrowroot, rice and more recently even barley. But in terms of the shape, Korean noodles have basically only two varieties – strips or strings.

So imagine my surprise when I found out, during my first travels to Italy in the late 1980s, that spaghetti and macaroni (or *maccheroni*, as the Italian name goes) are not the only types of noodle – or what they call *pasta* – eaten there. One particular shock was to be served *orzo* (or *risoni*) pasta in a summer school in Italy that I attended as a graduate student. *Orzo/risoni* is a pasta shape that looks like a small grain – the name literally means barley or rice – that is sometimes served in clear hot broth. When I was served it that way, I thought it was rice served in soup, as it is quite common in Korea to put your rice in hot (clear or otherwise) soup and eat them together. I couldn't believe it when I was told that I have just eaten a 'noodle' (pasta) dish.

In Italy, basically only one source of carbohydrate – wheat – is used to produce pasta (but see 'Acorn'). But over 200 varieties of pasta have been created by varying the shape. There are, of course, like in Korea and the rest of the world, pasta in the shape of strings or strips. But there are pasta that are made in the shape of tubes, rings, spirals/screws, butterflies, human ears, seashells, grains, balls, filled dumplings, sheets and many more obscure shapes (apparently – I haven't tried them – wagon wheels, olive leaves, spinning tops or even radiators).*

The Italian obsession with pasta shapes is such that in the early 1980s, Voiello, the premium brand of Barilla, the world's biggest pasta manufacturer, commissioned the famous industrial designer

---

* String-shaped pasta includes *spaghetti*, *bucatini*, *linguine*, *capelli d'angelo* (angel's hair) and *vermicelli* (little worms), while strip-shaped varieties include *fettuccine*, *pappardelle* and *tagliatelle*. *Penne*, *rigatoni* and *maccheroni* are tubes of various diameters and lengths. Ring-shaped ones include *anellini*, while *fusilli*, *trofie* and *gemelli* are spiral/screw-shaped. Butterfly (*farfalle*), human ear (*orecchiette*), seashell (*conchiglie*), grain (*orzo/risoni*) and ball (*fregola*) are also common shapes. The sheet-shaped one is *lasagne*, and filled dumpling-shaped ones include *ravioli*, *tortellini* and *mezzelune* (half-moon).

Giorgetto Giugiaro to come up with the ultimate pasta shape – a shape that would retain the sauce well without absorbing it too much, as well being decorative or even 'architectural' (this was time of *nouvelle cuisine*).[34]

Giugiaro literally 'engineered' a beautiful, futuristic pasta shape, made up of a tube combined with a wave. The shape was called Marille and was launched with a fanfare in 1983. Unfortunately, it was a total failure. The production run was limited, and the distribution poor, so it was difficult to get hold of. More importantly, the complex shape made it difficult to cook evenly.[35] Given the Italian passion for cooking pasta *al dente*,* unevenly cooked pasta was (almost) a cardinal sin.

Giugiaro obviously hasn't lost sleep over Marille's failure. He's been the world's most successful and influential car designer of the last half a century. He has designed over a hundred cars, for almost all the automboile manufacturers of international repute (General Motors, Mercedes-Benz and Nissan are the only exceptions) – ranging from dependable classics, like the Volkswagen Golf and Fiat Panda, to iconic luxury cars, like the Maserati Ghibli and Lotus Esprit. Judging from what he says about it, Giugiaro is taking the Marille debacle as an amusing interlude in his stupendous career. In a 1991 interview, he said: 'I owe my popular fame to that pasta, I got even published in *Newsweek*, isn't it funny?'[36]

Unbeknownst to most people, one of the earlier cars designed by this über-designer from the noodle-obsessed nation of Italy was Pony, a small hatchback car, launched in 1975 by Hyundai Motor Company, a then totally unknown car manufacturer from that other noodle-obsessed nation, South Korea.

Hyundai Motor Company (HMC) was part of the Hyundai business group, founded in the late 1940s by the legendary Korean entrepreneur Chung Ju-yung. The Hyundai group's main business was originally construction, but it started to move into higher-productivity industries in the late 1960s. Automobiles was the first

---

* Literally meaning 'to the tooth', as in firm to the bite.

of those ventures.* HMC was set up as a joint venture with Ford and assembled the Cortina car, developed by Ford UK, using mostly imported parts. In the first three years of operation (from November 1968), HMC managed to assemble just over 8,000 units of Cortina, that is, fewer than 3,000 cars per year.[37]

In 1973, HMC announced that it was going to sever its relationship with Ford and produce its own locally designed car – the Pony. In the first full year of production (1976), HMC produced just over 10,000 Pony cars – 0.5% of what Ford produced and 0.2% of what GM did in that year.[38] When Ecuador imported Hyundai cars in June 1976, the Korean nation was jubilant. The fact that Ecuador bought only five Pony cars and one bus from Hyundai was rarely mentioned and, if it was, dismissed as a minor detail; what mattered was that foreigners wanted to buy cars from Koreans – a nation of people who were then famous for producing wigs, stitched garments, stuffed toys, and sneakers – namely, things that require cheap labour.

Despite this totally inauspicious beginning, Hyundai grew at an incredible pace in the following years. In 1986, it made a spectacular entrance into the US market with its Excel model (an upgraded version of the Pony), which was named as one of the ten most notable products of the year by the US business magazine *Fortune*. In 1991, it became one of a handful of car manufacturers around the world that design their own engines. By the turn of the twenty-first century, it became one of the ten biggest automobile manufacturers in the world. In 2009, Hyundai (officially called Hyundai-Kia by then, having taken over its smaller domestic rival, Kia, in 1998) produced more cars than Ford did. By 2015, more cars with Hyundai or Kia marques rolled off production lines than did those branded by GM.[39]

It is an incredible story. If you had a time machine and went back

---

* Hyundai group subsequently diversified into cement, engineering, shipbuilding, steel, electronics, shipping, elevators, oil-refining, semi-conductors and many other high-productivity, high-tech industries.

to 1976 and told people that a totally unknown carmaker – really, little more than a glorified car mechanic's shop – from a poor developing country called South Korea, with a per capita income not even two-thirds that of Ecuador's,[40] was going to be bigger than Ford in just over thirty years and make more cars than General Motors in less than forty years, they would have tried to put you in a mental hospital.

How was this possible? When people hear about this kind of incredible corporate success, they immediately think of the visionary entrepreneur behind it – Bill Gates, Steve Jobs, Jeff Bezos, Elon Musk and the like.

And indeed behind the success of Hyundai there were two, not just one, visionary entrepreneurs – Chung Ju-yung, the founder of the Hyundai group, and his younger brother, Chung Se-yung, who led HMC between 1967 and 1997 (he played such a crucial role in the launch of the Pony that he earned the nickname, Pony Chung). When almost everyone else thought that there was a snowball's chance in hell that HMC would survive international competition, not to speak of becoming one of the top dogs in the industry, the Chung brothers worked with an ambitious vision to build a company that could one day globally compete, as symbolized by their decision to ask one of the world's best car designers, Giugiaro, to design their first car. They sank the money made by other more established (and profitable) parts of the Hyundai Group to sustain what was initially a loss-making company – this is known as intra-group cross-subsidization.

Important as these corporate leaders were, when you look more closely HMC's success story is not just – or not even mainly – about the individual brilliance of the heroic entrepreneurs.

First, there were the production-line workers, engineers, research scientists and professional managers in HMC who worked long hours, mastering imported advanced technologies, making incremental improvements on the mastered technologies and finally developing their own production system and technologies that can match those possessed by the world's top auto-makers, like Volkswagen and Toyota. Without a dedicated and capable workforce, corporate vision, however good it may be, remains just that – a vision.

And then there was the government. The Korean government created the space for the Hyundai and other carmakers to 'grow up' by banning the import of all automobiles until 1988 and the import of Japanese cars until 1998 (based on the logic of 'infant industry protection', which was also applied to other 'strategic' industries – see 'Prawn'). This of course meant Korean consumers putting up with inferior domestic cars for decades, but, without that protection, Korean carmakers could not have survived and grown. Until the early 1990s, the Korean government made sure that HMC and other firms in strategic hi-tech industries, especially export-oriented ones, had access to highly subsidized credits. This was accomplished through tight banking regulations, which mandated prioritizing lending to productive enterprises (over house mortgage loans or consumer loans), and through state ownership of the banking sector (see 'Acorn').*

The government policy was not always of the 'helping' kind. HMC's decision to design its own model was actually made because of the Korean government's 'domestication' programme for the automobile sector. In 1973, the government threatened HMC and other auto-makers that their licences to produce cars would be revoked if they didn't come up with their own models. Using its regulatory and financial power, the Korean government also put explicit and implicit pressure on HMC and other companies (foreign as well as national ones) to increase the 'local content' of their products – that is, the proportion of parts that were domestically

---

* All banks in the country were owned by the government between 1961 and 1983, and many of them remained in government hands until the early 1990s. Even today, there are still a few important state-owned banks – Korea Development Bank (specializing in large-scale lending over the long term), Export-Import Bank (specializing in trade credits) and Industrial Bank of Korea (specializing in lending to small and medium-sized enterprises).

produced – so that domestic car-parts industries would develop (see also 'Banana').

But, you may ask, isn't Hyundai's story an exception in a world of heroic entrepreneurs? The answer is that it is not.

To begin with, there are many other Korean companies that have succeeded in the same way as Hyundai, such as Samsung (from sugar-refining and textiles to world leadership in semi-conductors and mobile phones) or LG (from cosmetics and toothpaste to the top spot in the global display market).

Many of those Japanese multinationals that you have heard of have also developed along similar trajectories. Toyota started out as a manufacturer of simple textile machines and eventually became the biggest automobile manufacturer in the world, while Mitsubishi started out as a shipping company and became a multinational company spanning a huge range of industries, from shipbuilding and nuclear power plant to electronics and motor cars. All of them achieved such transformation through the combination of individual brilliance, corporate efforts, intra-business-group cross-subsidies, government supports and consumer sacrifice.

Nokia, the Finnish industrial giant, started out as a paper mill but grew into the one-time world leader in mobile phones and now a major force in network hardware and software through a similar formula. The Nokia electronics division, established in 1960, made its first profit in 1977, and had to be subsidized by other more established companies in Nokia business group (paper, rubber boots, electric cable) while receiving trade protection, restrictions on foreign investments and preference in 'public procurement' (government purchase of goods and services).

Even the US – a country that is so proud of its 'free enterprise' system and sings praises of heroic entrepreneurs all the time – has actually not been an exception to the collective nature of modern entrepreneurship. It is the country that invented the theory of 'infant industry protection' and erected a high wall of protectionism to create the space for its young companies to grow, protected from superior foreign, especially British, producers in the nineteenth and the early twentieth century (see 'Prawn').[41] More importantly for our discussion here, during the post-Second World War period, the US government critically helped its corporations by developing foundational technologies through public funding. Through the National Institutes of Health (NIH), the US government has conducted and funded research in pharmaceutical and bio-engineering. The computer, the semiconductor, the internet, the GPS system, the touchscreen and many other foundational technologies of the information age were first developed through 'defence research' programmes of the Pentagon and the US military.[42] Without these technologies, there would have been no IBM, no Intel, no Apple, and no Silicon Valley.

The individualist vision of entrepreneurship and corporate success that has been a central myth in the currently dominant free-market economics may have made some sense in the early days of capitalism, when scale of production was small and technologies were simple. In that environment, brilliant individual entrepreneurs could make a huge difference, although even in those days corporate success required more than individual brilliance alone. Since the late nineteenth century, with large-scale production, complex technologies and global markets, corporate success has been a result of collective – rather than individual – endeavour, involving not just corporate leaders but workers, engineers, scientists, professional managers, government policy-makers, and even consumers.

As the intertwined story of the two noodle-obsessed nations, Korea and Italy, shows, in the modern economy, entrepreneurship is not an individual deed any more. It is a collective endeavour.

7

Carrot

Carrot cake
Cake made with carrot, spices and nuts

When I first came to Britain, one of (many) things I found strange was carrot cake. Carrot was something to pickle with oriental cabbage in *kimchi*, boil with onions and potatoes in Japanese-style *karé* (curry), fry with other vegetables for *japchae** or put in salad. It was *not* for a sweet dish. Ever.

Carrot cake is now one of my favourite desserts, but initially it was like – I don't know – Brussels sprouts crumble for a Brit or broccoli pie for an American. It was just not a thing.

But when you think about it, the savoury-sweet division is rather culturally specific. Most people eat avocado as a savoury thing, but Brazilians often eat their avocadoes as desserts, with sugar. In most cuisines, tomato is a savoury ingredient, but, when I was young, in Korea, it was considered a sweet(-ish) thing. It was eaten as a fruit (which of course it is, in botanical terms), with added sugar if it wasn't sweet enough (which it often wasn't). Especially by the older generation, tomato was frequently called 'one-year persimmon', as it kind of resembles persimmon but, unlike the tree-grown persimmon, comes from an annual plant. Hence the name. Even after several years of living in the UK, where tomatoes were definitely savoury, it still rattled me to see a (great) 1991 American movie called *Fried Green Tomatoes* (you wouldn't fry persimmons, would you?).

*

* Korean glass noodles, or *dangmyun*, fried with julienne of vegetables, with shredded meat, if you want. See 'Noodle'.

56

Originally, carrots, which come from Central Asia (almost certainly today's Afghanistan), used to be white. Subsequently, purple and yellow varieties were developed. The now-dominant orange variety was developed in the Netherlands only in the seventeenth century.

It is widely believed that the Dutch promoted the new variety because it was associated with William of Orange (Willem van Oranje in Dutch) or William the Silent (Willem de Zwijger in Dutch), the leader of the sixteenth-century revolt against Spain, which was then ruling today's Netherlands. That, I guess, would make the carrot arguably the most political vegetable in history. Unfortunately, facts often get in the way of a good story: there seems to be no basis for this one.[43]

Beyond the politics of the Habsburg Empire and the Low Countries, the development of the orange carrot was genuinely significant in nutritional terms. The orange colour comes from beta-carotene, which the body turns into vitamin A when eaten. Vitamin A is essential for keeping your skin, immune system and especially eyes in good condition, so the orange carrot brought an additional nutritional benefit over its white ancestor. As with most vitamins, vitamin A will poison you if you have too much of it. This is known as hypervitaminosis A, which can lead to sluggishness, blurred vision, bone aches and, in extreme cases, peeling skin (eeeew!). Some early European polar explorers found this out to their horror when they ate the livers of seals – extremely rich in vitamin A – or of polar bears, whose main diet is seals.

Beta-carotene is a safe source of vitamin A which lets us avoid hypervitaminosis A, because the body regulates the amount of beta-carotene that is converted into the vitamin. Exploiting this fact, in 2000, a group of scientists led by Ingo Potrykus (Swiss) and Peter Beyer (German) transplanted two genes that can bio-synthesize beta-carotene (one from maize and another from a common soil bacterium) into rice and created the so-called Golden Rice. Golden Rice is rich in vitamin A, unlike natural rice, and has yellow-gold colour, thanks to the presence of beta-carotene.[44]

Rice is a very nutritious food, able to support more people than wheat in an equal land mass, but it is low in vitamin A. Poor people in rice-eating countries in Asia and Africa consume little else and therefore suffer from Vitamin A deficiency (VAD). VAD is estimated to be responsible for up to 2 million deaths, half a million cases of blindness and millions of cases of xerophthalmia, the debilitating eye-disease, every year. Golden Rice could potentially save millions of people from death and crippling diseases.

Soon after creating Golden Rice, Portrykus and Beyer sold the technology to Syngenta, a multinational agribusiness and biotechnology company. Syngenta, headquartered in the Swiss city of Basel, itself is a result of the corporate equivalent of genetic engineering at its most complex – it is the product of a series of mergers and acquisitions stretching back to 1970, involving three Swiss pharmaceutical companies (Ciba, Geigy and Sandoz), the British chemical giant Imperial Chemical Industries (ICI), the Swedish pharmaceutical company Astra, and the Chinese state-owned chemical company ChemChina.* Syngenta already had a legitimate partial claim on the technology thanks to its indirect funding of the research through the European Union, but it bought the scientists out and gained complete control over Golden Rice. The two scientists, to their credit, negotiated hard with Syngenta to allow poorer farmers in developing countries to use the technology for free.

Even so, some found the sale of such a valuable 'public purpose' technology as Golden Rice to a profit-making firm unacceptable. The scientists defended their decision by arguing that they would have had to negotiate licences for over seventy patented technologies,

---

* Ciba and Geigy merged to form Ciba-Geigy in 1970. Ciba-Geigy merged with Sandoz in 1996 to form Novartis. In 1993, the pharmaceutical and the agro-related businesses of ICI were separated to form Zeneca, which subsequently merged with Astra and formed AstraZeneca (of the Covid-19 vaccine fame) in 1999. The remainder of ICI was taken over by the Dutch chemical company, AkzoNobel, in 2008. In 2000, Novartis and AstraZeneca agreed to merge their agro-business operations, to form Syngenta. Subsequently, in 2016, Syngenta was taken over by China National Chemical Corporation (ChemChina).

involving thirty-two different owners, if they were to commercial-
ize Golden Rice themselves. They pointed out that they simply did
not have the capacity to negotiate and pay for the licensing of so
many patents. Critics retorted that it was really around thirty critical patents that the scientists needed to license.

However, the point remains – there were just too many patents
involved for individual scientists to handle. Unfortunately, despite
the patent issue being taken care of by a big multinational corporation (MNC), Golden Rice is, after two decades, still waiting for a
major roll-out due to controversies surrounding GMOs (genetically
modified organisms) in general. That is another story.

A patent is a government grant of a monopoly to the inventor of a
new technology over a fixed term in return for the inventor reveal-
ing the technology (that is, making it 'patent', i.e., obvious). A
patent is a double-edged sword in terms of its effects on the advancement of knowledge. It encourages the creation of new knowledge
by promising the inventors of (sufficiently novel) new ideas that
they will get the monopoly right to use their ideas for a period
(twenty years these days, although it used to be quite a bit shorter –
more on this later), which will enable them to charge whatever the
market will bear, with no fear of competition. However, it discour-
ages the creation of new knowledge insofar as it makes it impossible
for other people to use the technology concerned in creating new
knowledge during the period of monopoly.

The trouble is that the most important input in the production of
knowledge is knowledge, so, if a lot of pieces of relevant knowledge are patented, it becomes expensive to develop new knowledge,
as in the case of Golden Rice. This is what I call the problem of
'interlocking patents', also labelled 'patent thicket' by the eminent
economist Joseph Stiglitz.[45]

The problem of interlocking patents is not new. It paralysed
technological progress in the sewing machine industry in the mid-
nineteenth century. At the time, everyone in the industry was suing
everyone else for patent infringement, as their technologies were

closely related, thus halting the advancement of technologies. The solution to this stalemate was found in a 'patent pool' of 1856, in which the companies in the industry agreed to share the patents in all the key technologies and concentrate on developing new technologies; this was known as the Sewing Machine Combination. There have been many examples of patent pools created by the relevant industry – including DVDs (MPEG-2 or Moving Picture Expert Group-2) and mobile phones (RFID or Radio Frequency Identification).

Sometimes governments, especially the US government (that supposed supreme defender of patentee rights), have intervened to create a patent pool. In 1917, during the preparations to enter the First World War, in which aerial warfare was becoming important, the US government 'recommended' (read forced) a patent pool on the aircraft industry, including the then two biggest aircraft manufacturers, the Wright Company (established by the Wright Brothers) and Curtiss. In the 1960s, the US Navy, which had actually almost entirely funded the early researches on the semi-conductor, imposed a patent pool on Texas Instruments and Fairchild, the then leading manufacturers of semi-conductors.

The problem of interlocking patents has recently become far worse, as more and more minute pieces of knowledge, down to the gene level, have become patented, as we see in the case of Golden Rice (over seventy patents contained in a grain of rice!). Now you need an advance army of lawyers to clear the patent thicket, if scientists are going to make a major technological progress. In this way, the patent system, once a powerful spur to technological innovation, is turning into a major obstacle to it. We must reform it.

One way to improve the current patent system would be to shorten the life span of all patents. When first developed in Europe in the late eighteenth century, patents usually lasted for fourteen years (double the length of apprenticeship at the time). Today, patent protection lasts for twenty years, with the pharmaceutical industry getting up to eight years of additional protection on the grounds of the additional time needed for clinical trials and of the need to protect the data from the trials. There is no economic theory that says that twenty years (or twenty-eight years) is the optimal length of protection. Nor is there any theory saying that twenty years is better than fourteen years or, for that matter, ten years. If we shortened patent life, knowledge would get released into the public domain more quickly, dulling the innovation-hampering edge of the patent sword.

Another way to make the patent system less obstructive to the progress of knowledge is to use the prize system. Here, the inventor of a technology gets a one-off reward (proportional to its estimated usefulness), so the technology becomes a public property as soon as it is invented. The prize system was successfully used in the past to deliver some of the most important inventions in human history. John Harrison's invention in the 1760s of the marine chronometer, which enabled the measurement of longitude at sea and thus made accurate navigation possible, was partly a response to the prize of £20,000 offered by the British Parliament in 1714.[46] In 1809, Nicolas Appert, a French confectioner and brewer, invented the 'canning' technology (it was more a 'bottling' technology, as he used glass jars rather than tin cans, which came later; see 'Beef' on canning). This was in response to the prize promised by Napoleon, who wanted to feed his army properly – 'an army marches on its stomach', he is supposed to have said (although this was more probably Frederick the Great of Prussia).

In fields with rapid technological progress, the prize system may actually bring greater profits (and thus a greater incentive to innovate) to the innovator, as she does not have to worry about someone coming along with a better technology that makes her technology obsolete and destroys her market – in which case she may still have patent monopoly over her technology, but monopoly over nothing is still nothing.

We could also have an international agreement to force patentees to license their technologies at reduced prices if they are deemed necessary for developing public purpose technologies. In the case of the Golden Rice, Syngenta voluntarily ceased its commercial interest in it soon after it bought the technology – in 2001. As I write this chapter in the autumn of 2021, there is a debate going on as to whether pharmaceutical companies should be made to give licences to developing countries for their patented vaccines and treatments of Covid-19 at reduced prices – or even for free. Likewise, in light of the climate crisis, we must do the same for green energy and other technologies useful for adaptation to climate change (e.g., desalination of salt water). Developing countries do not have the capabilities to create these technologies, at least within the time that we have left (see 'Lime').

Like all institutions, we use the patent system because its benefits are greater than its costs. When this stops being the case, we should modify the institution, however outrageous the modified form may seem at first. After all, we eat the orange carrot today only because some Dutch person back in the seventeenth century had the ludicrous idea that carrots could be orange.

PART THREE

Doing Better Globally

8

Beef

Chilli Con Carne
(Mexican)
Beef (or turkey or meat substitutes) stew with tomato,
chilli, kidney beans and chocolate

Which is the best footballing nation in the world?

Many people would probably say Brazil, as it has won the most football World Cups – five. But how about Italy? It has won the Cup *only* four times, but with a population that is less than one-third that of Brazil's (61 million against 212 million).*

But it isn't even Italy. The correct answer is Uruguay.

Uruguay? Yes, that's right. It's the country that is known, at least in football terms, as the home of Luis Suárez, the brilliant footballer who is, bizarrely, notorious for biting other players.

Uruguay has only 3.5 million people and has won the World Cup twice. It won the first ever Cup in 1930 on its home turf, Montevideo. It then clinched it again in 1950, against the home team in the then Brazilian capital of Rio de Janeiro in arguably one of the biggest upsets in the history of football. If Uruguay had the population of Brazil, it would have won 121, not just two, Cups – that's 100 more than all the World Cups that have so far been won.

---

* Germany has also won the Cup four times. However, Italy still comes ahead, since Germany's fourth win was with a population significantly bigger than that of Italy's (over 80 million). Its three earlier wins (1954, 1974, and 1990) were as West Germany, which had a similar population to that of Italy's.

Two wins is a stupendous achievement for such a small nation, even if its first win was nearly a century ago and even its latest one was two generations ago (so, England fans, take comfort in the knowledge that there are other fans whose national team last won the Cup even further back in time than yours).

Incredible though this achievement is, football isn't the only field (no pun intended) in which Uruguay has excelled. It also has impressive records on matters of political and civic rights. In 1912, it became the first Latin American country where women won the right to file for divorce without a specific cause. It was one of the first countries in the world where women acquired the right to vote (in 1917). In 2013, it became the first country to legalize marijuana.*

Less glamorous than football, politics or civil rights, perhaps, the beef industry is another area in which Uruguay has been at the top of the international league. Currently, it is the country with by far the highest number of cattle per (human) capita.[47] It is not just the quantity but also the quality – Uruguay is the first country to have made every single one of its cattle traceable (in 2004).† Historically, Uruguay was the first country to mass-produce beef extract, which started out as beef stock reduced to thick liquid (thus also known as 'liquid beef') and later became the iconic beef stock cube, Oxo.

In 1847, Justus von Liebig, the German scientist known for his work on plant nutrition and considered to be one of the founding fathers of organic chemistry, invented beef extract. Liebig thought his extract would give access to the nutrients in beef to poor people who could not afford the real thing. Unfortunately for him, the raw

---

* However, I don't want to give the false impression that the country's always been on the side of the angels. It had a brutal military dictatorship between 1973 and 1985, during most of which José Mujica (president 2010–15), was a political prisoner.

† This is not to say that Uruguayan beef necessarily tastes the best. In my limited experiences, Argentinian beef tastes at least as good, if not better, than Uruguayan. I also have a very soft spot for the uniquely Brazilian cut of beef, *picanha*.

material was too expensive to make his extract affordable for most people, so it remained a culinary curiosity produced in small batches for the next fifteen years.

Then, in 1862, a young German railway engineer working in Uruguay, Georg Christian Giebert, learned of Liebig's invention. Giebert proposed to produce Liebig's extract in Uruguay, where (as in Argentina and Brazil) beef was very cheap, since it was essentially a by-product of the leather industry, because at the time it was impossible to export the meat to its potential markets in Europe and North America in the absence of refrigerator ships.*

In 1865, the Liebig Extract of Meat Company (LEMCO) was established in London. The production facilities were set up in the Uruguayan town of Fray Bentos (Friar Benedict in English), named after a seventeenth-century hermit who reputedly had lived in a nearby cave.[48] The Fray Bentos factory came with its own R&D (research and development) laboratory (which applied scientific knowledge to develop commercially viable products and production technologies), in those days a facility owned by only the most technologically advanced companies, like the German chemical giant BASF (see 'Anchovy').[49] Many historians consider LEMCO, subsequently with operations in multiple countries across the globe (in Europe, South America and Africa), to be the world's first multi-national food company (on multinational companies, or MNCs, see 'Banana').

LEMCO's beef extract was initially called – very imaginatively – Lemco (duh!). Despite having the lamest name in the history of human commerce, the product was a major hit worldwide. It provided a convenient and cheap way of making satisfying beef broth, if not supplying the nutrients that von Liebig initially had thought it would (it turned out that the extraction process removed most of protein and fat, and with them most nutrients).[50] The extract was

* Refrigerator ships were invented in the 1870s but they came to be deployed in large numbers only at the turn of the twentieth century.

made even more convenient when it was turned into a dried cube in 1908 and renamed Oxo.

Soon after its success with beef extract, LEMCO came up with another world-beating product – canned corned beef, which it started producing in 1873.

Corned beef – beef cured in salt – had been around for several centuries, if not longer, in Europe. But LEMCO made it accessible to a much larger proportion of humanity through the combination of cheaper ingredients and additional preservation technology. The cheap Uruguayan beef was made even cheaper by using less expensive cuts than the brisket, as in the 'proper' recipe, and mincing them (presumably to make it impossible to discern the less good cuts). By canning it, LEMCO made corned beef last much longer than the original salt-curing technology had allowed, and thus it could be exported over longer distances.

Oxo cubes and canned corned beef 'became staples for working-class people across Europe for whom meat had previously been a luxury item. They also provided inexpensive, long-lasting and easy-to-carry rations for British soldiers during the Boer War and British and German troops in the First World War, as well as for polar explorers like Robert Falcon Scott and Ernest Shackleton', in the words of Shafik Meghji, the award-winning travel writer reporting on the Fray Bentos World Heritage site* for the BBC.[51] Subsequently, during the Second World War, corned beef played a critical role in providing protein to British civilians as well as to soldiers. Between April and September of 1942, at the height of the so-called Battle of the Atlantic, during which a substantial portion of shipments of food from the US to Britain (and the Soviet Union) was

---

* In 1924, LEMCO was taken over by the Vestey Group (of Britain) and renamed Frigorífico Anglo del Uruguay (El Anglo for short), reflecting the fact that by then it was exporting a large amount of frozen and refrigerated beef (*frigorífico* means 'refrigerator' in Spanish). El Anglo remained a major force in the global food industry until the 1960s, after which it went into a decline. The complex that used to house the factories, laboratories, offices and living quarters of El Anglo, which ceased operation in 1979, was made a UNESCO World Heritage Site in 2015.

sunk by German U-boats (until the British cracked the supposedly uncrackable Enigma code of the German navy), canned corned beef made up one-seventh of the British meat ration.[52]

Corned beef isn't called that because it contains maize (or sweetcorn), which is what the word 'corn' means to most people these days. Corn as a synonym for 'maize' is the relatively new American usage. In the older British usage, the word means 'grain' – of any type, and not just maize.* The name 'corned beef' comes from the type of curing that produces it, which used to be done with 'corns' (that is, grains) of salt, although these days brine is typically used instead.

If they think about it, most Brits would realize that they have frequently encountered the old usage of the word, corn. Many of them live in a town with a building called the Corn Exchange, which is where the grain market used to be held in the old days (in the US, such a building would be called the Grain Exchange). Quite a lot of British people must have also learned about the Corn Laws in their history lessons in secondary schools.

The Corn Laws in question were introduced in 1815 to provide protection to British grain producers, such as import tariffs or an import ban on cheaper foreign grains. Although Britain had had numerous Corn Laws dating back to the fifteenth century, the 1815 legislation was particularly controversial because it came at the dawn of the Industrial Revolution, when manufacturing industries were expanding fast, and as a result the urban population was growing rapidly. To the city-dwellers (factory workers, clerks, shopkeepers and capitalists) who had to buy – rather than grow – their grains, the Corn Laws were an anathema.

---

* The changing meaning of the word 'corn' has created some mighty confusions. Some illustrations for the eighteenth-century novel *Robinson Crusoe*, which you can find on the internet, contain neatly planted rows of maize, when Crusoe talks of planting corns, which was really rice and barley in his case (see 'Coconut' for details of Robinson Crusoe's diet).

Without the Corn Laws, its critics argued, Britain could import cheaper foreign grains, enabling its urban population (and even many rural people who had to buy food, such as agricultural labourers) to eat more cheaply. With cheaper food, it was pointed out, capitalists would reap more profits, as they could pay lower wages for their employees, and thus be able to invest more in manufacturing industries, which were then propelling the country's prosperity. If this happened, the nation as a whole would be better off, even if it meant less rental income for agricultural landlords and lower profits for grain-growing capitalist farmers, the opponents of the Corn Laws argued.

The famous Anti-Corn Law League was formed in 1838 by two MPs (Members of Parliament), Richard Cobden and John Bright – who were among the political heroes of Margaret Thatcher, the former British prime minister known for her liberalizing zeal.[53] Backed by non-agrarian groups, whose number and power were swelling thanks to the Industrial Revolution, the League staged a highly effective campaign and managed to repeal the law in 1846.[54]

The repeal of the Corn Laws was 'the final victory' in 'the battle to end government restrictions on industry and trade', according to Milton Friedman, the best-known free-market economist of the twentieth century, in *Free to Choose*, his extremely influential book written with his wife, Rose Friedman. In the words of the Friedmans, the repeal 'ushered in three-quarters of a century of complete free trade lasting until the outbreak of World War I and completed a transition that had begun decades earlier to a highly limited government'.[55] According to the prevailing view on the history of capitalism, this 'liberal' international economic order, founded on free trade and free movement of capital under the leadership of Britain, resulted in a period of unprecedented global prosperity – until it got regrettably disrupted by the economic and political instabilities created by two world wars and the Great Depression.[56]

However, like all such stories, this 'origin story' of free trade is full of inaccuracies and myths. Let us put aside for the moment the fact that many of those 'government restrictions on trade and industry' that the Friedmans denounce as counter-productive were precisely what had enabled the global dominance of the British manufacturing sector in the run-up to the country's adoption of free trade (see 'Prawn').* Let us also ignore the 'detail' that Britain did not actually make a full transition to free trade with the repeal of the Corn Laws. Over 1,100 items were still subject to tariffs (many of them still very high) in 1848 – it was only by 1860 that Britain could be described as a truly free-trading nation, with fewer than fifty items subject to tariffs.[57]

Even if we ignore both these 'inconvenient truths', there is a glaring hole in the creation myth of free trade. It is that Britain wasn't actually even the first to practise free trade. That honour actually goes to the Latin American countries, which adopted free-trade policy a good few decades before Britain, between the 1810s and the 1830s.[58]

The Latin American countries may have been the pioneers of free trade, but their 'free' trade had *not* been adopted 'freely'. Upon gaining independence from their Spanish and Portuguese colonial masters in the first few decades of the nineteenth century, they had been forced by the European powers, led by Britain, to sign what came to be known as 'unequal treaties'. Among other things, these treaties imposed free trade on the weaker nations by depriving them of 'tariff autonomy', that is, the right of a country to set its own tariffs.† Only a very low uniform rate of tariff – usually 5%, but it could be as low as 3% – was allowed, so that the government could raise some revenue but not affect international trade flows.

---

* In 1860, Britain produced 20% of world manufacturing output, while in 1870 it accounted for 46% of world trade in manufactured goods.
† The most important among these 'other things' was 'extra-territoriality'. This meant that the citizens of the stronger countries could not be tried in the court of the weaker country because its legal system was judged to be of too low a quality for the citizens of the more 'advanced' countries. These treaties also involved giving concessions to individuals and companies from the stronger nations to exploit natural resources (e.g., mining rights, logging rights) at knock-down prices.

From the 1830s, other weaker countries that were still independent –
such as Turkey (then the Ottoman Empire), Thailand (then Siam),
Iran (then Persia) and China – were forced to sign unequal treaties
and made to join the band of free-traders. Japan also had to sign such
treaties from 1853, when it was forcibly opened up by the 'gunboat
diplomacy' of Commodore Perry of the US navy. When all those
treaties expired in the 1910s, Japan swiftly abandoned free trade and
jacked up its industrial tariffs to around the average of 30%, so that it
could promote its nascent industries against competition from superior foreign producers (see 'Prawn'). The Latin American countries
had already done the same when their unequal treaties expired in the
1870s and the 1880s.

While forced free trade was spreading around the globe throughout the nineteenth and the early twentieth centuries, protectionism
was the norm among the countries in Continental Europe (except
in the Netherlands and Switzerland) and North America.[59] The US
was a particular offender in this regard – it had average industrial
tariff rates around 35–50% between the 1830s and the Second World
War, which made it the most protectionist country in the world
during much of this period.

So, it turns out that the period that the Friedmans describe as
'three-quarters of a century of complete free trade' was not really a
period of 'free' trade as we normally understand it. Only a few (Britain, the Netherlands and Switzerland) among a couple of dozen
countries in Europe and North America that could choose their
own trade policies practised free trade. All the other free-trading
nations were doing so under compulsion, not out of free choice –
weaker nations in Asia and Latin America under unequal treaties or
the Asian and African colonies of European powers, which were
forced into free trade with their colonial masters.

Fortunately for the supporters of free trade, today's international trading system is not tarnished by these kinds of 'unfree free trade' any
more. The unequal treaties had all expired by the 1950s. By the 1980s,
most nations with a significant population had been decolonized,

although there are still surprisingly large number of territories under colonial rule (around sixty).[60] Most importantly, since 1995, international trade has been regulated by the World Trade Organization (WTO), in which all member countries have an equal voting right, unlike in all other international organizations, where countries with stronger military and/or economic power formally have a greater say.*

However, all of this still does not mean that there is no imbalance of power involved in international trade. Even though they don't exercise it as blatantly and brutally as before, stronger countries are still exercising their power to shape and manage the international trading system in their interests.

To begin with, the more powerful countries have had much greater influence in setting the agenda for the initial negotiations for the rules of the WTO and made sure that the rules were set in their favour. For example, the WTO puts fewer restrictions on trade protection and subsidies for agricultural producers than for manufacturing firms. It is not difficult to guess why – relatively speaking, rich countries have weaker agriculture and poor countries have weaker manufacturing. Or take the WTO rules limiting national governments' ability to regulate MNCs operating within their borders. The WTO bans the use of 'local contents requirement' (that is, a government requiring that MNCs buy more than a certain proportion of their inputs locally, rather than importing them – see 'Banana' and 'Noodle'). This rule disproportionately benefits rich countries because most MNCs are from rich countries. These examples show that, even if all countries abide by the same rules, the more powerful countries are likely to benefit more from the system because they have already ensured that the content of the rules favour themselves.

* In the United Nations, the five permanent members of the Security Council (the US, the UK, France, Russia and China) have veto power. In the World Bank and the IMF (International Monetary Fund) a country's voting right is linked to the share capital it has paid in, so rich countries have disproportionate power. As a result, the rich countries have the majority of votes while the US, with 18% of votes, has a de facto veto power over key decisions, as they require an 85% super-majority.

Moreover, written rules are one thing and how they are applied is another. Take the case of the WTO rules on tariffs, which in fact favour developing countries by allowing them to use higher tariffs. However, the benefits that developing countries derive from this rule are limited in practice because rich countries use their power to prevent them from fully employing their tariff allowances. This often is due to financial power. The rich countries have made trade liberalization a key condition for their financial support for developing countries – the bilateral 'foreign aid' they give and the loans disbursed by multilateral financial institutions, like the World Bank and the IMF, which they control (see footnote on p. 73). At other times, they use their 'soft power' (or, to use a fancier term, ideational power) – through the academia, international media, and policy think-tanks – to persuade developing countries that free trade is good for them. As a result, the *actually applied* industrial tariff rate of developing countries these days is around 10% on average, even though these countries are allowed to have tariff rates of 20%, 30% or even higher (depending on the country) according to the WTO rules. This shows that power does not just mean making someone do something against their will. It also means making others refrain from doing something in their own interests for fear of punishment from you or even in the belief that it is against their interests.

Thanks to the combination of a seemingly insatiable human taste for it and the developments of preservation technologies (extraction, canning, refrigeration), beef has come to conquer the world in the last century and a half.

Its dominance has been such that beef has turned the earth into 'the planet of cows', in the words of the straight-talking environmental scientist Vaclav Smil.* The beef industry is imposing huge environmental burdens on the planet in terms of greenhouse gases,

---

* According to Smil's calculation in a chapter titled 'The Planet of Cows' in his book *Numbers Don't Lie*, the zoomass of cattle is 1.5 times that of humans and 200 times that of elephants.

deforestation and water usage (also see 'Prawn' and 'Lime').[61] Beef has come to occupy such a dominant position in human food system that it is unthinkable to discuss the role of meat in human society and the economy, whether positive or negative, without talking about it.

Similarly, with the rise of capitalism and the accompanying ideology of free-market-free-trade economics, 'freedom' has become such a dominant concept in how we think about society and economy. Any idea that has the words 'free' or 'freedom' in it is considered good – free trade, free market, freedom of speech, free press, freedom fighters and so on. Anything that may be against these things, in turn, is considered primitive, repressive and backward-looking.

However, there are many different notions of freedom, and they cannot all be treated as being unequivocally good for everyone (see 'Okra'). In the case of 'free' in free trade, it only means freedom for those who are conducting trade across national borders not to be subject to regulations (e.g., import bans) or taxes (e.g., tariffs) by national governments. No more, no less. Hence the perverse situation like the first age of free trade (in the nineteenth and the early twentieth centuries), when 'free' trade was almost exclusively conducted by 'unfree' nations that had been deprived of the right to determine their own future through colonialism and unequal treaties. Even in a situation in which there is formal equality among nations, as in the current (second) age of free trade, free trade still does not mean that everyone benefits equally, as the rules of international trade are set and administered by stronger countries in their own favour.

Only when we understand the power imbalances that define international trade and do not get dazzled by the presence of the word 'free', can we understand why there are so many disputes and conflicts between nations about something that is supposed to be so unequivocally good for everyone as free trade.

9
Banana

Elvis sandwich, the Chang family version
(American)
Toasted bread topped with peanut butter and
sliced banana, drizzled with honey

There are a lot of dishes named after the person who (allegedly) invented them – such as Dongpo pork, Caesar salad and Nachos.* Or after the person whom they were (allegedly) invented for and dedicated to – such as beef Wellington, pizza Margherita and peach Melba.†

But there is one dish that is named after someone who was simply a fan of it: the Elvis sandwich. The Elvis sandwich, or just the Elvis, is a banana and peanut butter sandwich (often, but not necessarily, with bacon; sometimes with honey or jelly),‡ loved by Elvis Presley, the legendary American rock 'n' roll singer, or simply 'the King' to many people. Presley is supposed to have eaten it all the time, so much so that people came to call it after him.

I am with the King here. A peanut butter and banana sandwich, lightly drizzled with honey, is one of my wife's favourite breakfast

---

* After, respectively: the eleventh-century Chinese poet Su Dongpo; the early twentieth-century Italian-American chef Cesare Cardini; and the mid-twentieth-century Mexican chef Ignacio 'Nacho' Anaya.

† After, respectively: Arthur Wellesley, the first Duke of Wellington, the British general who beat Napoleon at Waterloo; Queen Margherita, the first queen of unified Italy (from 1871); Nellie Melba, the late-nineteenth-century Australian soprano.

‡ Jelly here is jam made after filtering out the fruit pulp after initial cooking, not the gelatine dessert.

items, and I often join her in the repast. The combination of the sweet, creamy taste of banana with the nutty, slightly salty taste of peanut butter is simply irresistible.

Having it as a sandwich filling, I admit, is rather an unusual way of consuming banana. People do use banana to make 'sweet goods' (like banana bread or banana muffins) or desserts (like the American banana split or the British banoffee pie). But the predominant form of banana consumption is to eat it as a fruit, like apple or straw-berry (well, it is a fruit, isn't it?), either 'neat' or as a fruit topping on breakfast cereals, yoghurts or ice creams.

That, however, is the case only for people who live in countries that don't produce bananas. It is estimated that 85% of bananas are con-sumed in places where they are produced – South and South-east Asia, Africa, South America and the Caribbean.[62] In these regions, bananas are of course eaten as a fruit, but, more often than not, they are cooked – as a carbohydrate component of a meal (boiled, steamed, fried, grilled, baked, you name it) or as a vegetable in savoury dishes (especially in southern India). And it is not just the so-called 'cooking banana', also known as plantain, that is cooked. It is also the case with the sweeter variety that is called 'dessert banana' (which is what people outside the banana-producing regions know as banana, since 95% of internationally traded bananas are dessert bananas),[63]* This is not surprising when the two types of banana are different cultivars of the same species and people in many banana-producing countries

---

* Almost all (95%) internationally traded bananas (and about half of all bananas produced worldwide) are of one variety, the Cavendish, even though there are over 1,000 varieties of banana around the world. The variety, developed in the mid-1830s, was named after William Cavendish, the sixth Duke of Devonshire. Cavendish didn't develop it himself – it was Joseph Paxton, his head gardener and friend, who did that. Paxton named the new banana variety *Musa cavendishii* (Musa being the genus that includes various species of banana) in honour of his employer and friend, as it was developed in the greenhouse in Chatsworth House, Derbyshire, the seat of the Cavendish family's dukedom (don't ask me why the seat of the Duke of Devonshire is in Derbyshire, not in Devonshire (or Devon) – there is no end to peculiarities and oddities in the world of British aristocracy).

often don't distinguish the two types from each other.[64] In many African countries, bananas are also brewed into beer. In the rural areas of countries like Uganda, Rwanda and Cameroon, banana can provide up to 25% of daily calorie intake.[65]

The banana is originally from South-east Asia. It is estimated to have been domesticated several thousand years ago.[66] In the process of domestication, in which seedless mutants were selected for having more edible parts, the banana lost its ability to reproduce by natural means. Domesticated bananas cannot be propagated without human intervention that involves 'the removal and replanting of vegetative cuttings of the offshoots (or suckers) that develop from the under-ground stem (or corm) of the mature plant'.[67] Bananas spread in such a way are, as a result, all genetically identical.*

The banana crossed the Indian Ocean and reached Africa sometime between the second millennium BCE and the first millennium CE (I know, it is a big timespan, but that is how it is with these things).[68] So, by the time the first Europeans, namely, the Portuguese, arrived in sub-Saharan Africa, on the west coast in the 1470s, bananas had been naturalized on the continent at least for several hundred years and possibly for millennia. The Portuguese adopted the word 'banana' from Bantu languages of West-Central Africa.[69] Ironically, the Europeans first encountered bananas in their ancestral

---

* This means that, compared to other crops, the banana can become genetically homogenous very quickly, especially in a commercial setting where profitability is the king. However, the resulting, limited gene pool makes it difficult to control diseases for the banana. Currently, there is a worry that the Cavendish banana, which accounts for 95% of internationally traded bananas, may be wiped out by so-called Panama disease, a wilting disease caused by a fungus. The banana industry is in this situation because it has repeated its historical mistake of reducing genetic diversity in pursuit of profit. Cavendish itself is a replacement variety that came on the commercial scene in the 1950s, when Gros Michel, which until then had been the absolutely dominant commercial variety, was wiped out by an earlier variety of the Panama disease (the TR One – or Tropical Race One – variety, as opposed to the current TR Four variety).

home in South-east Asia only in 1521, during the famous Pacific voyage by the Portuguese sea captain Ferdinand Magellan (or Fernão de Magalhães in Portuguese).[70]

The Portuguese used bananas to feed the enslaved Africans whom they were forcing to produce sugar on the island of Madeira and the Canary Islands (which were part owned by Portugal until 1479). When they started shipping Africans as slaves to the Americas, the Portuguese used bananas (especially plantains), together with rice, as a staple on slave ships. On plantations, the slaves were encouraged to plant bananas on the small plots given to them for the purpose of growing food to supplement their meagre rations. In the right climate, the banana plant grows all year around and is extremely productive, producing 200,000 pounds per acre – ten times the yield of yams and one hundred times that of potatoes – with minimal human labour input.[71] So it was an ideal crop for slave-controlled plots, on which the slave-owners wanted the slaves to spend as little time as possible.

The banana may have entered the Americas as an essential cog in the machinery of the slave-based plantation economy, but a few centuries later it became the engine of the export economy for many countries in the region.

In the late nineteenth century, the developments of railways, steamships and refrigeration techniques started to enable large-scale exports of perishable agricultural products over long distances (also see 'Rye', 'Okra' and 'Beef'). Banana was one of the major beneficiaries of this development. Due to their perishability, until the late nineteenth century bananas had been a luxury fruit sold in small quantities even in the US, which is quite close to the banana-growing countries in the Americas. Once the large-scale import of bananas into the US became a possibility, US companies, especially the United Fruit Company (Chiquita today) and its smaller rival the Standard Fruit Company (Dole today), established large-scale banana plantations in the Caribbean (Cuba, the Dominican Republic, Haiti), Central America (especially Honduras, Costa Rica, Nicaragua,

Panama and Guatemala) and northern South America (Colombia and Ecuador, which are the biggest banana exporters in the world these days).

The US banana companies soon came to dominate the economy of these countries. For example, in Honduras, the United Fruit Company (UFC) and the Standard Fruit Company (SFC) controlled the railways, electric lights, mail, telegraph and telephone.[72] In the 1930s, in Guatemala, UFC 'was the largest landowner, the largest employer, the largest exporter and the owner of almost all the country's railways'.[73] Many people in the banana-dependent countries called the US banana companies El Pulpo, 'the octopus', for having a tight grip over almost all aspects of their economies.[74]

Such near-absolute economic control naturally gave the banana companies an extremely high degree of hold over politics of the banana-producing countries in the Americas. Banana companies had their own customs and police, so much of their business was beyond national jurisdiction. Politicians were bought off, to guarantee 'pro-business' policies. Coups d'état against governments that tried to do things against their interests (e.g., raising extremely low taxes to very low levels, making them sell unused land, strengthening worker rights a tiny bit) were supported by the banana companies, sometimes reinforced by US mercenaries, called *filibusters* (derived from the Dutch word for pirates). Throughout the first half of the twentieth century, the US Marines regularly invaded and occupied some of these countries, in order to protect the interests of American companies, especially the banana companies.[75]

The US banana companies gained further notoriety with the so-called Banana Massacre in Colombia. In the autumn of 1928, the workers in UFC plantations went on strike, demanding things most of which would be considered essential these days: provision of toilets and medical facilities; payment of wages in cash, instead of coupons that could only be used in UFC shops selling goods at inflated prices; treatment of the workers as employees, rather than as subcontractors who could not even get the minimal protection that the weak labour laws offered.[76]* Under pressure from the US government, which threatened military intervention if the strike was not broken soon (all too credible, given its record in the region), the Colombian military decided to end it by forcible means on 6 December. In the process, it gunned down a large – and disputed – number of striking workers in the banana town of Cié-naga (the estimate ranges from 47 to 2,000).[77] The Banana Massacre has been permanently etched in our collective memory by Gabriel García Márquez, the Colombian novelist and a Nobel Laureate, in his masterpiece, *One Hundred Years of Solitude* (my favourite book ever, I must confess). In the book, García Márquez gives a fictionalized account of the event in which over 3,000 striking workers are killed, loaded on to rail carriages and taken away from the banana planta-tion of Macondo, the fictional town in which the novel is set, to erase all evidence of the massacre.

The dominance of the US banana companies in Central America and northern South America between the late nineteenth and the mid-twentieth centuries was such that these countries came to be called 'banana republics'. The term was coined by the American short-story writer, O. Henry (real name William Sydney Porter) in his 1904 short story 'The Admiral' set in Anchuria, a fictionalized version of Honduras, where he had lived in exile in 1897. In the story, which shows the pitiful nature of its government, both financially and organizationally, O. Henry calls Anchuria a 'banana republic'.[78] Some half a century later, in 1950, Pablo Neruda, the Chilean poet and another Nobel Laureate, added to the popularity of the term by writ-ing a poem called 'United Fruit Co.', in which he talks of 'banana republics'.

These days, many people in the US and other rich nations know the term 'banana republic' only as a clothing brand. But it was originally invented to describe the dark reality of the near-absolute domination of poor developing nations by large corporations from rich countries. The clothing brand name is at best ignorant and at worst offensive.

* So the gig economy wasn't invented in Silicon Valley.

It is like – I don't know – calling a hipster coffee grinding shop Satanic Mills or calling a luxury sunglasses store Dark Continent.

The phenomenon of the banana republic shows how powerful corporations from rich countries with operations in many countries – known as multinational companies (MNCs) or transnational corporations (TNCs) – can negatively affect the 'host economy' that receives their investments.

However, don't let that make you form a uniformly negative view of MNCs. MNC presence can bring a lot of benefits to the host economy.

Having MNCs around can enable economically backward economies to start an entirely new industry that they could not have dreamed of having on their own – as when, in 1998, Intel opened a new microchip assembly factory and started off the semi-conductor industry in Costa Rica, one of the original 'banana republics'.[79] Or indeed when the world's first semi-conductor companies, like Fairchild and Motorola, set up their assembly operations in the mid-1960s in South Korea – now one of the superpowers of the semi-conductor industry but then a poor country in which the assembly of transistor radios, mostly with imported parts, counted among the most advanced industries.[80]

Even in industries that already exist in the host economy, MNCs can teach superior technologies and new management techniques. This may happen directly, when the citizens of the host country work for MNC subsidiaries as managers, engineers and workers, and then move to local companies or even set up their own businesses, taking new knowledge with them. But it can also happen indirectly, when MNCs buy inputs from local firms, which then get to learn to meet higher technological and quality standards, sometimes with technical assistance from the MNCs.

So there can be huge potential benefits of having MNCs operate in your country. Citing these benefits, many business leaders, academic economists and international organizations, like the World Bank and the WTO, recommend developing countries to welcome MNCs with open arms, offer them low taxes or even tax exemptions,

regulate them lightly or even exempt them from some local regulations, especially regarding labour and the environment. Ireland and
Singapore are often cited as examples of countries that have been
able to achieve prosperity by actively hosting investments by MNCs,
known as FDI (foreign direct investment), through such policies.

The problem, however, is that these potential benefits from MNC
presence are just that – 'potential' benefits. Their realization requires
government policies that make MNCs behave in the right ways.

Given the relatively low level of skills that exist in developing
countries, MNCs draw from the international labour pool when
they hire for higher-level managerial and technological positions. As
a result, the locals in the host countries are left with low-level jobs,
with little scope for absorbing higher-level knowledge. In some
cases, for political reasons, MNCs may even bring their own people
for lower-level jobs too, as is the case with some Chinese construction companies. Given the low productive capabilities of local firms,
MNCs prefer to import inputs from their regular suppliers, back in
their home countries or countries where they have already established supplier networks, rather than trying the 'unknown quantities'
of local firms that are very likely to have to be taught new things.

The result is that the host country ends up with 'enclaves', iso-
lated from the rest of the economy, in which MNC subsidiaries
engage in 'screwdriver operations', just using cheap local workers
for final assembly with mostly imported inputs, buying little from
local firms. In such a case, there may be some limited short-term
benefits (such as wages paid to workers, some low-tech inputs
bought from local firms), but most of the real benefits from MNC
presence (such as transfer of better technologies, exposure to better
management practices, training of workers and engineers in more
advanced skills and technologies) do not materialize.

The most telling example of the 'enclave economy' is the Philippines, which, by some accounts, is literally the most hi-tech economy
in the world – it has the highest ratio of high-technology products
(mostly electronics) in its manufacturing export basket, at 60% (much

higher than the US at around 20% or even Korea at 35%), according to the World Bank data.[81] Despite being so 'hi-tech', the Philippines has per capita income of only around $3,500, as compared to over $30,000 in South Korea, not to speak of around $60,000 of the US. This is because the electronics products exported by the Philippines are all produced by MNC subsidiaries running screwdriver operations in economic enclaves. The Philippines may be one of the most extreme examples, but MNC subsidiaries in developing countries more often than not end up as screwdriver operations in enclaves.

Given this, it is not a big surprise that many governments have regulated MNCs in order to maximize the benefits from them. They have restricted the ownership share of MNCs, so that the MNCs have to go into a joint venture with a local partner, which will then have a much greater chance to learn from the better company than otherwise. In key sectors, the share was usually put under 50%, so that the locals have a better bargaining position. Countries have required MNCs to transfer technology to their subsidiaries or put ceilings on the royalty they can charge for licensing their technologies to the subsidiaries. They have sometimes mandated MNCs to hire more than a certain proportion of the locals in the workforce, or to train workers they hire. To maximize the indirect benefits of MNC investments, they have required the MNC subsidiaries to buy more than a certain proportion of their inputs from local suppliers – this is known as the 'local contents requirement'. These policies were used extensively – and successfully – by countries like Japan, South Korea, Taiwan and Finland between the end of the Second World War and the 1980s.[82]

The cases of Korea and Taiwan are particularly interesting. In attracting MNCs, they initially offered tax breaks and even partial suspension of already weak national labour laws in sectors that did not involve high technologies (garments, stuffed toys, trainers, for example). However, contrary to prevailing opinion today, they imposed all sorts of regulations to direct MNC investments into hi-tech industries, like electronics and automobiles, and to extract the largest possible amounts of technologies and skills from MNCs.

Thanks to these policies, Korea and Taiwan now possess some of their own world-class MNCs, like Samsung (Korea) and TSMC (Taiwan) in semi-conductor production, LG (Korea) in display and Hyundai-Kia (Korea) in automobiles (see 'Noodle'). China has been doing similar things in the last few decades, although its large domestic market (which most MNCs were dying to tap into) gave it such a bargaining leverage that much of knowledge transfer were arranged through informal negotiations with individual MNCs, rather than through formal legislation, as in the cases of Korea and Taiwan.

Even Ireland and Singapore, which most people assume have succeeded economically because they had been liberal with MNCs, actually have done so because of public policy intervention (their strategic locations – Ireland's EU membership, Singapore's location at the key node in international trade – also helped). Their governments went out of the way to provide custom-made supports to MNCs that were willing to invest in high-technology industries, like electronics and pharmaceuticals, rather than simply waiting for any MNC to turn up and do whatever it wanted.[83] In the case of Singapore, the government also made the most of its position as the country's supreme landlord (owning almost 90% of the land) in attracting MNCs in high-productivity industries, by offering them good locations at reasonable rents.

The banana is the most productive fruit in the world. But that productivity, used in the wrong way, has led to highly negative outcomes. It was initially used to keep the slaves in the Americas alive at minimal costs to plantation owners. Later, it became the cause of labour exploitation, political corruption and international military invasion in many economies around and in the Caribbean Sea.

MNCs are like that. Like bananas, many of them are highly productive. However, if they are used in the wrong way, the host country will end up as an 'enclave economy', if not a 'banana republic'. Only when there are public policies to ensure maximum transfer of technologies, worker skills and management practices, will host economies truly benefit from the presence of MNCs.

10

Coca-Cola

Coca-Cola
(American)
You know what it is

I cannot say I am a regular drinker of Coca-Cola – or any other type of cola.

But, sometimes on a hot summer afternoon, even for me, there is nothing like an ice-cold Coca-Cola. Except that I won't drink it straight from a bottle or a can. This is not because I am particular about drinking etiquette. It is just that I need a container – I could drink it from a bowl if need be. The thing is that I want to drink Coca-Cola, even if it has been chilled, with (lots of) ice cubes in it, as I find the drink too sweet on its own and need to have it diluted.

But billions of people on the planet disagree with me. They love what to me is the overly sweet taste of Coca-Cola. According to the British journalist Tom Standage, writing in the mid-2000s, there are 'two hundred territories where the Coca-Cola Company operates – more than the United Nations has members. Its drink is now the world's most widely known product, and "Coca-Cola" is said to be the second most commonly understood phrase in the world, after "OK".'[84]

Being arguably the most iconic American product, Coca-Cola has come to symbolize American capitalism, and what is good and bad about it. For some, like dissident youths in the former Soviet Union, Coca-Cola was a symbol of freedom – personal, economic and political.* For others, like the left in India until the 1980s, it

---

* I shouldn't overstate the symbolic importance of Coca-Cola. It was arguably the

epitomized what is wrong with American capitalism – consumerism and, worse, commercial manipulation of consumer taste. In 1977, in a highly symbolic move, the Indian government cancelled the licence for Coca-Cola to operate in the country when the company refused to go into a joint venture with a local partner. Equally symbolically, the company came back to India in 1993, soon after its economic liberalization in 1991. Few food items have been laden with so much political symbolism on a global scale as Coca-Cola.

One person who deftly negotiated the symbolic minefield that is Coca-Cola is Marshal Georgi Zhukov, who masterminded the Soviet victories over the Nazis in the crucial Second World War battles of Leningrad and Stalingrad. He is said to have been introduced to the drink by the American general (later president) Dwight Eisenhower during the war and fallen in love with it. While he was serving as the commander of the Soviet occupation forces in Europe (May 1945– June 1946), he made a special request to the Coca-Cola company to manufacture a clear version of the drink, so that he could have it without being seen to be imbibing the essence of American capitalism. The white version, which was created by taking out the caramel colouring, was produced in Brussels, put in a nondescript bottle and shipped to the Marshal's European headquarters.[85] A brilliant manoeuvre worthy of one of the greatest military strategists in history.

Coca-Cola was first invented by John Pemberton of Atlanta, Georgia, in the US.[86] In 1885, he launched Pemberton's French Wine Coca, whose main ingredients were coca leaf, kola nut and wine. There had been other drinks that mixed alcohol and coca leaf. Particularly popular was Vin Mariani, a wine in which coca leaves had been steeped for six months, whose fans included Queen Victoria and Thomas Edison.[87] Pemberton's innovation was to add kola nut to the mixture. The drink was sold as a 'nerve tonic' (whatever that

---

most important symbol, but also iconic were Levi's jeans, Marlboro cigarettes and LP records of rock 'n' roll bands.

actually means – there seem to have been a lot of nerve problems around in the nineteenth-century Western world).

In 1886, alcohol was prohibited in the then main market of Pemberton's drink (Atlanta, Georgia, and the surrounding Fulton County). Pemberton took the alcohol out of his French Wine Coca and added sugar (to mask the bitter taste of the two principal ingredients, coca leaf and kola nut, which became too prominent without the taste of wine) and citrus oils. The resulting non-alcoholic drink was called Coca-Cola.

Coca-Cola was initially sold in drug stores from a soda fountain, possibly to add to its medicinal credentials, as carbonated drink was at the time considered to have health benefits. It began to be bottled in 1894, thus allowing long-distance shipment and thereby greatly enlarging its potential market. By the mid-1910s, it had become so popular that there were counterfeits, which the company tried to repel by running an advertising campaign saying, 'Demand the genuine.'[88] The company started exporting the drink in the 1920s. By the 1930s, Coca-Cola had become a national icon. In 1938, it was described as 'the sublimated essence of America'.[89]

The name Coca-Cola was invented by one of Pemberton's business partners, Frank Robinson, who named the drink after the two key ingredients – *coca* leaf and *cola* (kola) nut.

Kola nut originates in West Africa. It contains stimulants, like caffeine (which it contains more than coffee and most teas) and theobromine (which is also contained in chocolate – see 'Chocolate').[90] Given this property, West Africans have chewed it in order to stimulate themselves and also to suppress appetite, thus enabling its consumer 'to undergo prolonged exertion without fatigue or thirst'.[91] The chewing of kola nut plays an important role in community meetings, rites of passage and ceremonies to cement treaties and contracts in West African cultures.[92] It is also said that kola nut made the foul, stale water on long-distance crossings more palatable and for that reason was used by slave ships coming from Africa.[93]

Kola nut in Coca-Cola was replaced by a synthetic chemical in 2016.[94] This has made the drink like one of those ageing rock bands which, after so many line-up changes over the years due to artistic differences and clashes of egos, have no original members left any more. Coca Cola's other founding member, coca leaf, which used to provide cocaine (to add to caffeine and theobromine from kola nut), had already 'left the band' more than a hundred years ago in the early twentieth century, when the company decided to take it out of the formula when cocaine's addictive quality became clear.*

Cocaine is derived from the coca plant, which is native to western South America. Especially in the high-altitude Andean region of its habitat, coca leaves have been chewed or brewed as tea by indigenous people, to relieve pains while working in the oxygen-poor atmosphere and to help themselves go on without food, as coca leaves reduce appetite (in the same way that kola nuts do).[95] These forms of coca plant consumption are not addictive or harmful to health and, more importantly, like the shared chewing of kola nut, they play important cultural and religious roles in Andean and other indigenous communities in Latin America.[96] Many people there grow coca plants.

Evo Morales, the former Bolivian president (2006–19) and the second-ever indigenous president of a Latin American country (after Benito Juárez, the nineteenth-century Mexican president (1858–72)), was a coca farmer himself. He came to political prominence through his campaign against the forcible eradication of coca farming, which the Bolivian government was pursuing in the late 1990s and the early 2000s with strong US government support, as part of the latter's 'War on Drugs'.

In 2005, Morales became the president on the wave of protest against the so-called 'Washington Consensus' policies of fiscal retrenchment, trade liberalization, deregulation and privatization, which had ill-served his country in the preceding two decades. The Washington Consensus policies are so named because they are advocated by

---

* To be more precise, coca leaf is still in the band but only as a ghost. Since it decided to take out cocaine from the drink, the company has been using 'spent' coca leaves, from which cocaine has been completely extracted, only as a flavouring.

the three most internationally powerful economic organizations headquartered in Washington, DC, namely, the US Treasury, the International Monetary Fund (IMF) and the World Bank.

Upon becoming president, Morales nationalized the natural gas industry, the country's main export industry. He then went on to (at least partially) nationalize the 'utilities' (electricity, water and railways), raised the royalties that (mostly foreign) mining companies paid to the government (as the guardian of the national mineral wealth) and increased social welfare spending. Many economists predicted his changes would lead to a dire economic disaster – nationalized industries, hostile policies towards foreign investors and 'downward' income redistribution being the worst things that a government can do for the economy, according to the Washington Consensus.

But Bolivia's performance defied the sceptics. Given Morales's policies, it was natural that the country saw a dramatic fall in income inequality during his term.* But the country's economic growth also accelerated markedly – the growth rate of its per capita income rose from 0.5% per year during the period of Washington Consensus (1982–2005) to 3% per year during the Morales era.

Bolivia isn't the only country in Latin America that has defied the Washington Consensus and improved its economic performance. Between the late 1990s and the mid-2000s, leftwing or left-leaning parties came to power in several Latin American countries – Argentina, Brazil, Ecuador, Uruguay and Venezuela – in what is known as the Pink Tide.†

---

* Bolivia's Gini coefficient (a common way of measuring a country's income inequality, with a higher number denoting greater inequality) fell from 0.57 to 0.48 between the two periods, according to the data from the World Bank and the Economic Commission for Latin America and the Caribbean (ECLAC) of the United Nations. I thank Mateus Labrunie for the collection and the processing of the data.
† The relevant presidents were: Néstor Kirchner and Cristina Fernández in Argentina; Luiz Inácio 'Lula' da Silva and Dilma Rousseff in Brazil; Rafael Correa in Ecuador; Tabaré Vásquez, José Mujica and Tabaré Vázquez again in Uruguay; and Hugo Chávez and Nicolás Maduro in Venezuela.

None of them went as far as Bolivia, but the Pink Tide governments rolled back many of the 'neo-liberal'* policies of the
Washington Consensus. They increased welfare spending for the
poor, while some of them increased minimum wages and strength-
ened trade unions, thereby increasing the share of national income
going to workers. Some of them also partially reversed trade liberalization, increased subsidies to selected industries and toughened
regulations on foreign investors (see 'Banana').

Their policies defied the prediction by the neo-liberal orthodoxy
and brought about both greater equality and faster growth. The
exception is Venezuela under the uniquely disastrous presidency of
Nicolás Maduro. There the economy has collapsed; but Venzuela's
economic performance under his predecessor, Hugo Chávez, while
not being as impressive as in other Pink Tide countries, was still an
improvement over the neo-liberal policies of the previous era.[†]

I am not saying that everything was going well in the Pink Tide
countries. Inequality, while falling in most of them, remained still
very high by international standards. More importantly, the Pink
Tide governments didn't try hard enough to develop a solid basis
for sustained economic growth by developing high-productivity

---

* Neo-liberalism is a post-1980s version of nineteenth-century classical liberalism,
which had gone into retreat between the First World War and the 1970s. Both
versions of liberalism, classical and 'new', advocate strong protection of private
property, minimal regulation of markets, free trade and free movement of capital. The new version, however, is not as openly opposed to democracy as the old
one was (which argued that democracy will allow non-propertied classes to destroy private property and thus capitalism) while also, differently from classical
liberalism, opposing free markets in things like currency (it advocates a strong
central bank, which has monopoly over currency issue) and ideas (it advocates a
strong protection of intellectual property – see 'Carrot').

† Per capita income stagnated in Venezuela during the Washington Consensus era
(1989–99). It grew at 1.3% per year during the Chávez era (1999–2012), while
income inequality, with a Gini coefficient at around 0.45, stayed the same between
the two eras. The data are from the same sources as those in the footnote on p. 90.

industries that could replace their traditional natural resource-based industries, such as mining and agriculture, whose long-run growth potentials are limited (see 'Anchovy'). The biggest failure in this regard was Brazil. Brazil's 'Pink Tide' governments of 'Lula' (Squid!) Da Silva and Dilma Rousseff largely continued with the liberal trade and industrial policies of the neo-liberal era and let its once-mighty manufacturing industry decline beyond repair. By the end of the Pink Tide period, Brazil became more dependent on exports of natural resources (e.g., iron ore, soy beans, beef) than it had been during the peak neo-liberal era.*

Given their failure to reduce their dependence on primary commodities, the 'Pink Tide' countries were hit hard when the global commodity price boom of the 2000s, which had been fuelled by China's super-growth, came to an end in 2012–13. As a result, all these governments, except the Venezuelan one (which descended into a bizarre travesty of socialism under the autocratic rule of Nicolás Maduro) lost power in elections during the second half of the 2010s, except in Bolivia, where it was through a coup d'état.

However, changes of government did not lead to the the restoration of a neo-liberal *ancien régime*. In Argentina and Bolivia, Pink Tide parties took back power after a short interlude.[†] As I write in the spring of 2022, many commentators are predicting that a Pink Tide government could win again in Brazil's 2022 presidential election, following the disastrous presidency of the rightwing Jair Bolsonaro and the return of the former president, Lula, to politics.

Moreover, in the late 2010s and the early 2020s, some Latin American countries that had not joined the Pink Tide started to move to the left. In Mexico and Peru, left-leaning Andrés Manuel López Obrador

---

* Brazil's manufacturing sector, which accounted for around 30% of its national output in the late 1980s declined to just above 10% by the end of its Pink Tide.

† Alberto Fernández in Argentina took back the presidency in 2019 after one term, while Luis Arce in Bolivia won the presidential election in 2020, after one year of interim presidency by Jeanine Añez, who had been installed by the coup d'état.

and Pedro Castillo took the presidency in 2019 and 2021 respectively. In June 2022, Gustavo Petro was elected the first ever leftist president of Colombia.

The most significant in this regard is the victory of Gabriel Boric, a thirty-five-year-old former student activist, representing Frente Amplio, or the Broad Front, that is, the coalition of leftwing parties, in the Chilean presidential election of December 2021. Since the military coup in 1973, Chile had been the trailblazer for neo-liberalism not just in Latin America but in the world, even anticipating the neo-liberal policies of Margaret Thatcher and Ronald Reagan in the 1980s (see 'Okra'). So when Chile elected Boric as the president, who had declared that 'Chile was the birthplace of neoliberalism, and it shall also be its grave!', it was as if Americans had voted to ban Coca-Cola. Perish the thought . . .

The rejection of the neo-liberal Washington Consensus policies has been less visible in other parts of the developing world, such as Asia and Africa.

In Asia, it was mainly because the countries in the region had not followed the Washington Consensus policies in the first place as rigidly as did the Latin American countries. Their generally good economic performance has meant that relatively few Asian countries have had to borrow heavily from the Washington institutions, making it less necessary for them to adopt neo-liberal policies. Moreover, many Asian countries have had a less ideological approach to economic policies, so, even when they adopted neo-liberal policies, those policies were usually not implemented in their extreme forms, as they were in Latin America.

The African countries, even though they have suffered even more than did the Latin American countries from the Washington Consensus policies,* have found it more difficult to openly reject them,

---

* Per capita income in the Sub-Saharan African countries grew at 1.6% per year during the 1960s and the 1970s, but it grew as 0.3% between 1980 and 2018. In Latin America, the growth rates were 3.1% and 0.8% respectively.

given their greater dependence on the Washington institutions for financing. Even so, in the last decade or so, there has been an increasing recognition across the African continent of the need for a much more active role for the state than what is recommended by the Washington Consensus.[97]

Neo-liberal policies have not worked well even in the rich countries. During the neo-liberal period since the 1980s, these countries have had slower growth, higher inequality and more frequent financial crises than they had in the preceding decades of the 'mixed economy', in which the government played a more active – that is, more intrusive, from the neo-liberal point of view – role in restraining and regulating market forces.*

However, neo-liberal policies have been positively disastrous for developing countries because they were particularly unsuited to their needs. Above all, the neo-liberal orthodoxy denied the fact that developing countries can develop their economies only if they can create the 'space' for their producers to 'grow up' and acquire the capabilities to engage in higher-productivity industries through trade protection, subsidies, regulation of foreign investors and other supportive government measures (see 'Prawn' and 'Banana'). To make it worse, especially in the 1980s and the 1990s, the Washington institutions' policy recommendations took what came to be derogatorily known as a 'cookie cutter' approach, in which the same set of policies was recommended to all countries, regardless of the differences in their economic conditions and socio-political environments.

The continued success of Coca-Cola shows that a successful product requires happy customers, even if there is a minority of customers who are not entirely happy with it (like me). Unable to make its customers happy, the Washington Consensus policy package, once so dominant in the developing world, looks set to disappear into the twilight of history.

* See my earlier book, *23 Things They Don't Tell You About Capitalism*.

PART FOUR

Living Together

II

Rye

Mackerel with tomato salsa on rye crispbread
(my recipe)
Rye crispbread topped with tomato salsa (chopped-up parsley,
tomato, olive and chilli, with a dash of fermented anchovy sauce)
and grilled mackerel fillet pieces

When I decided to pursue my graduate studies in Britain in the mid-1980s, most Koreans, including my parents, were puzzled, to put it mildly. At the time (as it still does, albeit a little less), studying abroad for Koreans meant studying in the US. You just didn't go to other countries, especially Britain, which was considered to be a country in decline and didn't even have any historical links with Korea (as my country had been deemed unworthy of the British Empire's famously acquisitive attention).

I wanted to study in Britain because I was disillusioned by the rather narrow, technical Neoclassical economics I was being taught in my undergraduate programme in Korea. At the time (sadly, rarely any more), British economics departments offered a more pluralistic approach to economics than did their US counterparts – offering education in Keynesian, Marxist and other schools of economics – so Britain looked to me to be a better place to study economics in a broader way.

When I gave this reason to economists, teachers and friends alike, most of them told me that I was committing career suicide – even before it had begun. But it was too complicated to explain to non-economists, so I came up with a pat answer if they asked why: I am a huge fan of 'deduction novels' – the literal translation of *choori-sosurl*, the Korean name for detective novels – and Britain is where the best deduction novels come from. This seemed to stop most people from asking any further questions, even if I could tell that they thought me weird.

I was introduced to detective fiction as a young boy through the Sherlock Holmes stories of Arthur Conan Doyle. Many of his short stories, like 'The Red-Headed League', struck me with the ingenuity of their plots, while horrifying scenes from novels like *The Sign of Four* and *The Hound of the Baskervilles* haunted me. In secondary school, I read over one hundred classic 'deduction novels' – Maurice LeBlanc (his Arsène Lupin stories are having a brilliant and ingenious revival with the Netflix series *Lupin*), Ellery Queen, Georges Simenon, Raymond Chandler, G. K. Chesterton and others.

The undisputed monarch of the genre for me, however, was Agatha Christie – as she is for many people – her two billion book sales providing proof. Over the years, I have come to love a broader range of crime and spy novels than classic puzzle-solving detective fictions, devouring the works of authors like John Le Carré, Jo Nesbø, Andrea Camilleri and Fred Vargas, but after nearly half a century and several repeat readings, I still get jolts from the paradigm-shifting plot devices and narratives of Christie classics like *The ABC Murders, Murder on the Orient Express, 4:50 from Paddington, And Then There Were None* and *Five Little Pigs*.*

Among my favourite Agatha Christie stories was *A Pocket Full of Rye*, featuring Miss Marple, the harmless-looking spinster whose shrewd observation, sharp wit and profound understanding of human psychology make her a most formidable sleuth (although Hercule Poirot, the arrogant, hyper-rational but compassionate Belgian detective with an excellent moustache, is still my favourite). The story itself was ingenious, but I was also intrigued by the title. Never mind the nonsensical nature of the nursery rhyme, 'Sing a Song of Sixpence', from which the title is derived (like quite

* This is not one of the most well-known of her works, but it is one of my favourites. I think it is unfairly undervalued.

a few other Christie titles), but what was rye, or *homil* in Korean, I wondered?

Homil means 'northern nomads' wheat' – *mil* meaning wheat and *ho* being a prefix that we Koreans put on anything that we think (sometimes wrongly) came from nomadic peoples of Central and Northern Asia – so we are talking about a huge swath of the Eurasian continent, stretching from Manchuria, through Mongolia and Tibet, down to Uzbekistan and Turkey. So I knew that rye is something similar to wheat, but I had no idea what it actually was, never having eaten anything made with the grain.

Once I was in Britain, I *had to* eat rye – I couldn't let myself remain ignorant of the grain that is a key plot device in one of my favourite detective stories. Ryvita, the British rye crispbread, was the first thing I got to try. I really liked the nutty and slightly sour taste of rye and frequently ate it as a late-night snack when I was 'burning the midnight oil' as a graduate student. Then there were various rye breads. I found dark rye breads, like the German *pumpernickel*, a bit too dense for my taste but loved the lighter ones, especially those with caraway seeds. Later, during my visits to Finland, I grew to love Finnish rye crispbreads, especially the ones mixed with pine bark flour (which used to be a famine food; Finland is actually the last European country to have experienced famine – during 1866–8), which make you feel like you are standing in a slightly chilly northern forest.

Rye is originally from modern-day Turkey, but it has come to symbolize the Northern European food systems – a hardy grain that grows in the harsh northern climes where its more delicate cousin wheat cannot. Russia claims the title of the biggest consumer of rye, while Poland has the highest per capita consumption and is also the biggest exporter of the grain. But the world champion of rye is Germany, producing the largest amount of the grain, 33% more than the next biggest producer, Poland.[98] Rye is so important for Germany that it even features prominently in its historiography.

The 'marriage of iron and rye' is the nickname for the political

alliance brokered by Otto von Bismarck, the first chancellor of unified Germany, between the *Junkers*, the landed nobility mainly based
in Prussia, and the newly emerging capitalists in 'heavy' industries,
concentrated in the Rhineland in the west.

In 1879, Bismarck ditched his longstanding coalition partner since
the German unification of 1871, the National Liberals, who supported,
among other things, free trade. He forged a new protectionist power
bloc by getting the politically powerful rye-producing *Junkers* accept
tariff protection for the Rhenish heavy industries, like iron and steel,
then struggling against superior British producers. In order to do
that, he offered the *Junkers* tariff protection against cheap American
grains that were beginning to flood into the European markets,
thanks to the increased settlement of the North American prairie
(think the 1970s US TV drama *Little House on the Prairie* – also see
'Okra') and the development of railways that could bring the grains
from the prairie to the main seaports on the East Coast.

This alliance between the rye producers and the iron producers,
brokered by the 'Iron Chancellor', propelled the German economy
to new heights. It allowed the new heavy industries – iron, steel,
machinery, chemicals – to grow behind protective walls and eventually catch up with the leading producers in Britain, even though it
meant more expensive food than would have been under free trade
in agriculture (but then most people had a higher income as a result
of Germany's more successful industrialization, so higher food
prices did not matter much).

Bismarck's legacy didn't end with the development of German
heavy industries. There is another legacy of his that has had even an
bigger impact – and far beyond Germany: the establishment of the
welfare state.

Many people think that the welfare state is the product of 'progressive' political forces, like the New Deal Democrats in the US, the
British Labour Party or the Scandinavian social democratic parties,
but it actually was the arch-conservative Bismarck who created it first.

In 1871, soon after unifying Germany, which had until then been divided into dozens of political entities (around 300 if you go back further, to the eighteenth century), Bismarck introduced an insurance programme protecting workers from industrial accidents. Although it covered only a limited range of workers, rather than being a universal scheme, it was the world's first public insurance for working people.

Once he consolidated his power with the 'marriage of iron and rye' in 1879, Bismarck accelerated his push for welfare measures and introduced public health insurance in 1883 and a public pension in 1889 – both unprecedented anywhere in the world. In 1884, he extended his earlier industrial-accident insurance to cover all work-ers. Germany didn't quite manage to introduce the first-ever unemployment insurance (that honour goes to France), another keystone in the modern welfare state, but Bismarck can be credited for establishing the first welfare state in history.*

Bismarck didn't introduce the welfare state because he was a 'socialist', as anyone supporting the welfare state is apt to be called these days. He was a famous anti-socialist. Between 1878 and 1888, he maintained the so-called anti-socialist laws that heavily restricted the activities of the Social Democratic Party, although they fell short of banning the party altogether. But he was acutely aware that, unless workers were given protection against major shocks of life (industrial accidents, illnesses, old age, unemployment, etc.), they would be attracted to socialism. In other words, Bismarck initi-ated those welfare schemes that many people these days consider 'socialist' in order to keep socialism at bay.

Exactly for this reason, many socialists, especially in Germany, were against the welfare state in the beginning. They saw it as a way of 'buying off' workers and stopping them from overthrowing cap-italism through a revolution and establishing socialism. However, over time, reformist tendencies beat revolutionary ones within leftwing movements, and parties on the left came to accept and actively push for the expansion of the welfare state, especially

---

* Germany introduced unemployment insurance in 1927, by which time several countries had introduced it, starting with France in 1905.

following the Great Depression. After the Second World War, even many centre-right parties in European countries came to embrace the welfare state, as they realized that giving security to ordinary citizens was vital for achieving political stability, especially in the face of systemic competition from the Soviet bloc countries.

It is not just in terms of its origin that the welfare state is misunderstood. So is its very nature.

The most common misunderstanding about the welfare state is that its main function is to give 'free' stuff to poorer people – income support, pension, housing subsidies, healthcare, unemployment benefit and what not. These 'freebies' are, it is believed, paid for by the taxes that richer people pay. It is seen as a vehicle for poorer people to free-ride on richer people, as expressed in the increasingly common British expression 'welfare scroungers', which is used in order to denounce welfare recipients.

However, welfare benefits are *not* free. Everyone pays for them. Many of the welfare benefits people get are financed by 'social security' contributions – that is, payments tied to specific public insurance schemes against things like old age and unemployment – that most taxpayers pay. In addition, most people pay income tax, although poorer people pay a lower proportion of their incomes in income tax than richer people do (unless they live in a country that has a 'flat tax'). Moreover, even the poorest people who are exempt from income tax or social security contributions pay 'indirect taxes' when they buy things – value-added tax, general sales tax, import tariffs and so on.[99] In fact, these taxes are proportionately much more burdensome on the poor. For example, in the UK, as of 2018, the poorest 20% of households paid 27% of their income in indirect taxes, while the richest 20% paid only about 14%.[100]

Understood this way, no one is getting 'free' stuff through the welfare state.* If anything *looks* 'free', it is because it is 'free at the

---

* Unless they are corporations that pay their workers below the living wage, making it necessary for those workers to rely on the welfare state for survival, while

point of access'. For example, in Britain, thanks to socialized health provision under the NHS (National Health Service), you don't have to pay each time that you go to hospital. But you have paid for your hospital visit (and will keep paying for it in the future) through your taxes and social security contributions.

The welfare state is better seen as a package of social insurances, covering eventualities that can happen to anyone, collectively purchased by all citizens. It may (but may not, depending on how the tax system and the welfare schemes are designed) have an element of downward redistribution of income, but that is not even its main role.

The point of the welfare state is that, as citizens (and long-term residents), we all get the same package of insurances at a lower price by buying in bulk. The best way to illustrate this point is to compare healthcare cost in the US, which is the only rich country that does not have universal public health insurance, with that in other rich countries.

As a proportion of GDP, the US spends at least 40% more and up to two-and-a-half times more on healthcare than other similarly rich countries do (17% of GDP against the range of 6.8% for Ireland to 12% for Switzerland).[101] Despite this, the country has the worst health records in the rich world, meaning that 'health' is far more expensive in the US than in other rich countries. There are various explanations for this,* but one important reason is that the American healthcare system is fragmented and thus cannot benefit from collective purchases as much as its counterparts in other countries that have a more unified healthcare system. For example, each hospital

---

not paying their fair share of taxes by booking their income in tax havens.

* For example, higher income inequality in the US creates, proportionally, a larger group of people with greater stress and poor diet. Higher inequality also creates stronger 'status anxiety', which has negative health impacts, according to the famous book *The Spirit Level* by Richard Wilkinson and Kate Pickett. The greater power of the processed food industry makes Americans eat more unhealthy food. The way American cities are built results in more 'food deserts', with limited access to affordable and nutritious food.

(or hospital group) has to buy its own medicines and equipment, rather than buying them through a national system that benefits from 'bulk buy' discount, while each medical insurance company (as well as charging higher premium, being a profit-seeking entity) has to have its own system of administration, rather than a unified one that benefits from 'scale economy'. Some of you may not be convinced of this 'collective cost-saving' argument, but, if you have participated in collective purchase schemes, like Groupon, you have already bought into the idea behind the welfare state.

The welfare state has become the most effective way of dealing with the inevitable insecurity that capitalism creates in its pursuit of economic dynamism. Moreover, if designed well, the welfare state can make capitalist economies even more dynamic, as it reduces people's resistance to new technologies and new working practices – the Nordic countries are the best examples of this (see 'Strawberry').[102] No wonder that the welfare state has been spreading and growing, despite the continuous attack on it by neo-liberal ideology since the 1980s.*

People in today's rich countries owe their security – and prosperity – to a humble, hardy grain that is often considered inferior to its better-known cousin, wheat. For without protecting the rye produced by Prussian landlords, Bismarck could not have forged the political alliance that enabled him to build the first welfare state in the world.

---

* In 1930, the welfare state (or more technically, social spending, which includes income support for the poor, unemployment benefit, pensions, health and housing subsidies) typically accounted for 1–2% of GDP in today's rich countries, with Germany having the biggest one at 4.8%. By 1980, these countries were spending 15.4% of GDP on social spending on average. Today (the 2010–16 period), the corresponding figure is 20.8%.

12

Chicken

Grilled harissa chicken with vegetables
(my recipe)
Pieces of chicken, aubergine, courgette and onion,
marinated in harissa, olive oil and salt and then grilled

Poor chicken. No one takes it seriously. I know of no culture which venerates it, as Hindus do the cow. Neither is there a culture that denigrates it, in the way Muslims and Jews do the pig. Chicken is not even disliked properly. There are people who would shun certain meats not out of religious or cultural taboos but out of distaste – Hindus can but often won't eat pork, while many Koreans simply won't eat lamb, despite having no food taboo about it. But anyone who is willing to eat meat seems willing to eat chicken.

This universal acceptability of chicken may be partly because of the relatively low profile of the creature itself – a small, relatively docile bird, not a hulking animal (like cows, horses or pigs) or a hardy, obstinate creature (like sheep or goats). But it must mainly have to do with its versatility as a source of protein, with its rather neutral taste and with the relative ease of cooking. And indeed it is cooked in every conceivable way – deep-fried (American southern fried chicken, Japanese *tori kara-age*, Korean *yangnyum* chicken), shallow-fried (Chinese, Thai and many other national dishes that are too numerous to name), stewed (French *coq au vin* or North African chicken *tagine*), roasted (various European versions of roast chicken or South Asian *tandoori* chicken), flame-grilled (Malay or Thai chicken *satay* or African-Portuguese *piri-piri* chicken), smoke-grilled (Jamaican *jerk* chicken), boiled (Korean *sam-gye-tang* – boiled chicken with glutinous rice and ginseng roots – or

Jewish chicken soup), you name it. I have even eaten chicken *sashimi* in a restaurant in Japan, every single one of whose dishes was made with chicken.

Given its status as *the* universal meat, it is not a surprise that chicken is the choice of airlines, which have to cater for so many different food preferences and taboos in a confined space. Aeroflot, the Russian airline, seems to have had taken this policy to the extreme during its Soviet days.

When I was a graduate student in Cambridge in the late 1980s, an Indian friend of mine used to fly home with Aeroflot, via Moscow. Apparently the airline was awful in every conceivable way (comfort, punctuality, attitude of the cabin crew and so on), but many Indians stoically endured it, as their tickets were by far the cheapest. According to my friend, sickly white, goose-bumpy, tasteless chicken was the only inflight meal available. On one of his Aeroflot flights, my friend overheard a fellow Indian passenger ask a stewardess whether he could have something other than chicken – because he was, well, a vegetarian. In response, the stewardess quipped: 'No, you cannot. Everybody's equal on Aeroflot. It's a socialist airline. There's no special treatment.'

The stewardess's response was of course an extreme version of the Soviet principle that everyone should be treated equally, because everyone is a human being who is equally valuable. So, whether someone was a government minister, a medical doctor, a coal miner or a cleaner, each person would be given the same ration of bread, sugar, sausages, an annual pair of shoes and everything else through collective provisions. No special treatment.*

---

* That was the theory. The practice was rather different. Not only were there substantial pay differentials between different people (although much smaller than those in capitalist countries), but the political elite did get special treatment – better housing, access to special stores with better (often imported) goods, and opportunities to travel to capitalist countries (where they could, among other things, buy luxury goods not available to ordinary people back home).

There is a serious problem with this way of approaching equality and fairness.

It is true that, as human beings, we all have the same 'basic needs'; we need clean water, we need safe shelter, we need nutritious food. In that sense, the socialist principle is an important indictment of the practices in feudal and capitalist societies, where some people starve to death while others wallow in luxury. However, once we depart from the basics, our needs begin to diverge pretty quickly, and treating everyone in the same way becomes problematic.

Take the case of bread – a staple food item in many societies. Giving everyone the same amount of bread per day may sound fair in times of grave food shortage (such as in the Soviet Union during the post-agricultural-collectivization shortage of 1928–35 or the UK in the post-Second World War shortage of 1946–8). However, it isn't fair if the bread is leavened wheat bread, which some people simply cannot eat – perhaps because they have coeliac disease, perhaps because they are Jews observing Passover. For another example, providing male and female toilets of the same size in a public building may sound even-handed, given that roughly half the population is male and the other half female, but it is a very unfair thing, as women need more time and space in the toilet – hence the snaking queues outside female public toilets in cinemas, concert halls and other venues.

In short, treating people with different needs in the same way – giving vegetarians chicken, giving coeliacs wheaten bread, allocating the same toilet space to women as men – is fundamentally unfair. Unlike what the Aeroflot stewardess thought, treating people with different needs differently is not giving them special treatment. It is one of the most important conditions of fairness. In offering vegetarian options in in-flight meals, providing gluten-free bread or making female toilets more numerous, we are not showing favouritism to vegetarians, coeliac sufferers or women, respectively. We are simply putting them on an equal footing as the others in their fulfilment of basic needs.

*

Interestingly, those at the other end of the political spectrum from the socialists, namely, free-market economists, have an equally blinkered view of equality and fairness, albeit in a totally different way.

Free-market economists argue that the socialist system didn't work because it tried to ensure low inequality by paying everyone similarly (it was never the 'same', except in extreme cases like Maoist China or Cambodia under Khmer Rouge), despite the fact that different people make vastly different contributions to the economy. There are inventors, investment bankers, brain surgeons and entertainers, the free-marketeers point out, who make huge contributions to the economy. As for the rest, most people are competent at what they do while there are some who are suited only for the most basic jobs. In such circumstances, they argue, trying to achieve low inequality by paying people within a narrow range spells disaster. This is not only unfair for the more capable people who are rewarded less (sometimes far less) than their contributions merit but it is also socially counter-productive because it makes the more capable people less motivated to work hard, invest and innovate. This can only bring equality in poverty, free-market economists opine.

Therefore these economists assert that we should let individuals compete to the best of their abilities and accept the outcome of the competition, even if it produces a distribution of income that may seem excessively unequal according to some views. This is the most productive and the fairest system, they say: the most productive because individuals will have the highest incentive to maximize their outputs, the fairest because they will be rewarded according to their contributions to the economy.

The validity of the principle of paying people according to their contributions has an important pre-condition. It is that everyone has the chance to try for the best possible jobs – namely, there should be equality of opportunity.

This is not a trivial condition. In the past, many societies placed formal restrictions on people's choice of education and occupation because of caste, gender, race and religion (see 'Acorn'). The Universities of Oxford and Cambridge did not accept non-Anglicans (e.g., Catholics, Jews, Quakers) until 1871 and didn't award degrees to women until 1920 and 1948 respectively.* Under Apartheid in South Africa, Blacks and 'coloureds' (the Apartheid term for people with a mixed ethnic background) were forced to study at severely under-funded and crowded non-white universities, making it almost impossible for them to get decent jobs.

Today, most of these formal discriminations have been abolished, but no country has achieved true equality of opportunity. Women in workplaces are not given the same opportunity as men based on the sexist view that women are less likely to put career above family, if not the mistaken and downright offensive view that they are inherently inferior to men. Racial discrimination in education, the job market and the workplace is still rampant in all multi-racial societies, which give greater opportunities to less able people from ethnic-majority backgrounds over more capable ones from minority backgrounds.

The discrimination may even be partly self-imposed. In many societies, some subjects are widely considered to be 'masculine' – science, engineering, economics – and a lot of bright young women 'voluntarily' choose not to study these subjects even when their aptitudes may make them entirely suitable.† In my undergraduate programme in economics in South Korea in the early 1980s, there were only six female students in the cohort of 360 or so, while the engineering school had only eleven female students among a cohort

* Non-Anglicans were admitted to the Universities of Oxford, Cambridge and Durham only after 1871. Women were allowed to study in Oxford and Cambridge from the late nineteenth century, but they were not awarded degrees until 1920 in Oxford and 1948 in Cambridge.
† However, there is a considerable variation across countries. Engineering is one of the most male-dominated subjects, but 50% of engineering graduates are women in Cyprus, while the figures are 36% and 38% in Denmark and Russia. In Korea and Japan, it is just 5–10%. The data are from UNESCO (United Nations Educational, Scientific and Cultural Organization).

of over 1,200.* There was no formal rule that female students could not study engineering or economics, but many bright female students chose to study 'feminine' subjects like English literature or psychology, because they had been socialized to think those suited them better.†

In other words, if some people are prevented, formally and informally, from even entering the competition for the best educational places and jobs due to characteristics that have nothing to do with their capabilities for those jobs (such as gender, religion and race), the outcome of the competition cannot be seen as being the most productive or the fairest one. Equality of opportunity is vital.

Now, let us suppose that, in some future society (hopefully not too far into the future), we somehow achieve true equal opportunity for everyone to compete. Also, let us also assume that everyone is playing by the same rules (in practice, rules are often rigged – just think about 'legacy' students in American universities, who get advantage in admissions because their parents or grandparents attended the universities they are applying to). Can we then say that we should accept whatever inequality exists in such a society, because everyone has had the same chance to compete in the same game according to the same rules?

Unfortunately, even then, we cannot.

This is because everyone having equal opportunity to compete under the same rules does not mean that the competition is truly

---

* I am glad to report that these days, the proportion of female students in economics in my old university is over 30%, approaching 40%, while even the engineering school has seen the proportion rising to around 15%. Still not good enough, but much better than forty years ago.

† Emphasizing self-censoring is not to say that these choices are entirely, or not necessarily even mainly, due to the individual female students 'internalizing' sexist social norms. Some of those who chose not to study 'masculine' subjects may have been overruled by their parents, while others may have been afraid of disapproval from their relatives and friends. I thank Pedro Mendes Loureiro for raising this point.

fair. We don't call a race fair simply because everyone starts from the same starting line if some runners have only one leg or are blind in one eye.* Likewise, in real life, the fact that everyone in theory has the same opportunity to try for any job they like does not make the competition fair, if some contestants lack the minimum necessary capabilities; some may have had their brain developments stunted due to childhood malnutrition while others may have had sub-standard education because they grew up in deprived areas with below-average educational funding. In other words, equality of opportunity is meaningless unless every member of society has the minimum necessary capabilities to make use of the opportunity.

So, if we are going to make the race of life truly fair, we need to ensure that all children develop minimum capabilities before they join the race. This requires that all of them get adequate provision of nutrition, healthcare, education and playtime (whose importance in child development is increasingly recognized). This, in turn, requires that the differences in circumstances among those who are raising children – parents, relatives and guardians – should not be too large. That is, unless we are going to raise all children in collective creches, like in Aldous Huxley's *Brave New World* or in North Korea today (although even there, I am told, there are superior creches for the political elite). In other words, equality of opportunity is not enough; we need a relatively high degree of equality of outcome.

Greater equality of outcome may be achieved through regulations of markets. Some regulations protect the economically weak from

---

* Indeed, in real-life sports, we take the differences in potential contestants' capabilities extremely seriously and do all kinds of things to create genuinely fair contests. Not only do we have Paralympics, we have gender division, age groups and weight classes. Especially in sports with weight classes, such as boxing, wrestling, taekwondo and weightlifting, the view on what is a fair contest can be extremely strict. For example, in lighter classes of boxing, the weight band is 3–4 pounds, or 1.5–2 kilograms, meaning that we think a guy who is more than a couple of kilos heavier beating up the lighter guy is so unfair that we don't even allow them to fight in the same ring.

the strong. For example, Switzerland and South Korea lower their income inequality by protecting small farms (e.g., by restricting agricultural imports) or small shops (e.g., by restricting large retailers). Lower inequality could also be achieved through financial regulations (e.g., restricting high-profit but high-risk speculative activities) or labour market regulations (e.g., enforcement of a decent minimum wage, increases in sick pay). However, as we can see in the cases of highly equal European welfare states, greater equality of outcome is more effectively achieved by redistribution through the welfare state – whether it is through direct income transfers or through guaranteeing equal access to quality 'basic services', such as education, healthcare and water (see 'Rye').

The debate on inequality has been conducted in a misleading way for too long because people have only thought of outcomes and opportunities, while neglecting needs and capabilities. The left has thought that equalizing the outcome for everyone is the fair thing to do, ignoring that different individuals have different needs and capabilities. The right has believed that equality of opportunity is sufficient, without realizing that truly fair competition requires some equality in capabilities among individuals, which cannot be guaranteed without a considerable degree of equality in outcome among their parents' generation, achieved through income redistribution, guarantee of access to quality basic services and regulation of markets.

We don't want to fly with an airline which thinks giving chicken to vegetarians is fair. However, neither do we want to fly an airline which offers a range of meal alternatives catering for different tastes and needs (and even perhaps more than one type of chicken dish?) but only at the cost of a ticket that few of us can afford.

13
Chilli

Chilli kimchi
(Korean, my mother-in-law's recipe)
Green chillies pickled in red chilli powder, chopped garlic
and myulchi-jut (*Korean fermented anchovy sauce*)

A lot of people are, understandably, scared of the hot taste of chilli. To those who are not used to it, its fiery flavour can be a source of a range of discomforts – burning mouth, watering eyes, pain-induced sweating and even intestinal cramps. For people from what I call the 'Chilli Belt', ranging from Mexico (where the name 'chilli' comes from), Peru, the Caribbean Basin, Northern Africa, South Asia, South-east Asia, China and up north to Korea, the idea of eating food without the sharp pleasure from the heat of chilli is unthinkable.

The hotness of chilli is not really a taste but a pain. It is actually a chemical trickery of the highest sophistication, conjured up by the berry (yes, it is a berry in disguise – see 'Strawberry'). Despite the burning pain it causes, especially to our membranes, capsaicin, the main source of the hot taste in chilli, does *not* actually cause any direct tissue damage. It just fools our brain into believing that our body is undergoing such damage. It does so by binding itself to one of our sensory receptors that 'enables the body to detect extremes of temperature, the contact of acidic or corrosive substances, or the effect of any kind of abrasion or chafing'.[103]

Chilli's hotness is such an issue that a dedicated scale has been invented to measure it. It is called the Scoville Scale, after Wilbur Scoville, an American pharmacist, who, in 1912, came up with the idea. It measures the 'heat' of a chilli by extracting the heat components (capsaicinoids) of it by dissolving a dried specimen in alcohol, diluting it with sugared water and letting a panel of five tasters decide whether they can feel the heat.[104] According to the system, if the majority (that is, three out of five) of the tasters cannot detect the heat when one part of a particular chilli is diluted to, say, 10,000 parts of water, the chilli will get a Scoville Heat Unit (SHU) of 10,000.*

Not as discerning as the Scoville scale, but a more intuitive chilli scale has evolved among restaurants serving food from the Chilli Belt in countries where native food is mild, to help their customers avoid chilli-induced pains. The scale has zero to two or three pictures of chillies next to the dishes in the menu, denoting their chilli contents.

A Sichuan restaurant in London that I visited with my friend Duncan Green, the renowned development campaigner,† in the early 2000s deployed a rather extended chilli scale; its chilli signs ranged from zero to five. Most Sichuan dishes contain chilli in some form (fresh, dried, ground, pickled, as well as being added in the forms of chilli bean paste and chilli oil),[105] so the restaurant must have felt that it needed a finer scale than the usual two or three chillies in order to properly distinguish its dishes from one another in terms of hotness.

As a good Korean, I wanted go all the way up to portions with five chillies, but I checked myself and ordered options with fewer chillies, for Duncan could not take too much chilli heat. Duncan,

---

* Bell peppers have a SHU below 100, *cheongyang* chilli (a hotter variety of Korean chilli) ranges between 10,000 and 25,000 SHU, Thai bird's-eye chilli is between 50,000 and 100,000 SHU. *Habanero* chillies, depending on the variety, range between 100,000 and 750,000 SHU. The Carolina Reaper, with up to 2.2 million SHU for the hottest specimen, has been recorded as the hottest chilli in the world by *Guinness World Records*.

† Duncan is also a pioneer in the emerging field of 'science of social change'. See his books *From Poverty to Power: How Active Citizens and Effective States Can Change the World* and *How Change Happens*.

while being excited by the challenge of spicy flavours, ordered a dish with no chilli sign as an insurance. I agreed that it was a wise move – if worst came to worst and he found the other dishes too hot, he would have at least one to enjoy.

When the food arrived, however, Duncan blanched. His 'no chilli' dish had five or six pinkie-sized fried dried chillies in it. Utterly baffled, he asked the waitress whether there was a mistake. The waitress said that there was no mistake, and, when Duncan protested that he had ordered a dish without any chilli, she explained that a dish having no chilli sign next to it didn't mean that there was no chilli in it. The chilli sign was, she explained with the patience of a schoolteacher trying to explain something to a particularly slow child, just an indicator of relative hotness, not the indication of the amount of chilli in it.

Accepting his fate, poor Duncan took out the chillies from his dish but some of the capsaicinoids were already in the food, making it still a little too hot for him. As for the other dishes, to his credit, he tried all of them and liked them, albeit with some sweat and tears.

The story has a happy ending. Duncan grew to like the taste of chilli and kept going back to the restaurant, which eventually became one of his favourites.

When something is ubiquitous, it is taken for granted. And when something is taken for granted, it does not get counted, like chilli in the 'chilli scale' of the Sichuan restaurant in my story. The supreme example of this category in economics is the unpaid care work done at home or in the community.

The most widely used measure of economic output, Gross Domestic Product, or GDP, counts only things that are exchanged in the market.[106] Like all other measures in economics, it has its problems, but the biggest problem is that it is based on a very 'capitalist' view that, given how different people value the same thing differently, the only way to decide how valuable something is to the society is to see what price it commands in the market.

This practice of counting only marketed activities makes a huge chunk of economic activities invisible. In developing countries, this means that a big share of the agricultural output is not counted because a lot of rural people consume at least a part of what they produce. Since this proportion of agricultural output is not exchanged in the market, it does not get captured in GDP statistics. Both in rich countries and in developing countries, this market-based measure of output means that unpaid care activities, done at home or in local communities, are not counted as a part of national output – child-bearing, child-rearing, educational help to children, care for the elderly and the disabled, cooking, cleaning, laundry and household management (which involves what the American sociologist Allison Daminger calls 'cognitive labour').[107] These activities are not counted despite the fact that they would amount to 30–40% of GDP, if valued at market prices.[108]

The absurdity of not counting non-marketed care work can be seen if you do a simple thought experiment.* If two mothers swapped their children and took care of each other's child, while paying each other the (same) going rate for childcare (which will leave both of them financially unaffected), GDP will increase, even if the amount of childcare remains the same.† At a more conceptual level, it is deeply problematic not to count those activities without which human society, not to speak of the economy (which is nestled in society), cannot exist in the first place.

Given that the vast bulk of unpaid care work is done by women, not counting it means a big undervaluation of women's contribution to our economy – and society. This 'invisibility' of household work is such that we talk of 'working mothers', as if mothers who stay at home do not 'work'. This reinforces the sexist prejudice that women do nothing when they are at home, when the amount of labour put into care work at home is often much larger than what

---

* I haven't invented this thought experiment, but I cannot remember where I saw it first.
† Better still, these mothers can increase GDP even more simply by charging each other more.

their male partners put into their paid employment. We should refer to 'working' mothers as those 'in paid employment' as a step towards giving full social recognition to unpaid care work.

Undervaluation of care work is not just a matter of social recognition. It has material consequences for women. Women tend to take on caring roles (ranging from child-bearing and -rearing to taking care of sick or elderly relatives) more often and thus spend less time in paid employment than men do. Since pension entitlement (beyond basic state pension) is tied to one's wages, this means that, other things being equal, women cannot accumulate as much pension entitlement as men can, although in some European countries this is partly (but only partly) addressed by measures like 'care credits' for time spent on childcare and eldercare.[109] This, in turn, greatly increases the chance of women who devote time to unpaid care work ending up in poverty in old age.

It is not just unpaid care work but also paid care work that is undervalued, compared to the contribution that it makes to society. We saw this in the most stark and tragic way during the Covid-19 pandemic.*

During the pandemic, many countries realized that, like those who are doing unpaid care work at home and in communities, there are some people without whose work our very existence as society is impossible. These included those who are doing paid care work – in medical professions (e.g., doctors, nurses, ambulance drivers), childcare, senior care, teaching and so on. They also included those whose work is not care work per se but is necessary for the survival and the renewal of society ('social reproduction' is the technical term) – those who produce food and other essential items, those who distribute them (e.g., supermarket workers, delivery people), public transport workers, those who clean and repair buildings and

---

* The World Health Organization (WHO) declared the outbreak of Covid-19 a Public Health Emergency of International Concern on 30 January 2020, and a pandemic on 11 March 2020.

infrastructure and so on. People who work in such professions were designated 'key workers' in the UK and 'essential employees' in the US and were given 'privileges' regarding things like basic shopping or education of their children.* They were even hailed as 'heroes'.

One thing that emerged from this experience was that almost all those 'essential' workers, with the exceptions of top medical doctors, are poorly paid. Now, this is something of a paradox. If some activities are essential, shouldn't those who are engaged in them be paid the best, by definition?

One reason for the undervaluation of even marketed care work is the same as what is behind the neglect of unpaid care work – that is, the deep-rooted practice of gender discrimination. For a number of reasons, which one chapter cannot encompass, women, especially women of colour and immigrant women, are disproportionately represented in low-paid caring professions – nursing, childcare, old-age care-home services and domestic services.[110] These female workers are not only paid less than their male colleagues doing similar jobs, but they are paid much lower wages than what male workers with comparable abilities would be paid in male-dominated professions. In other words, women's work is undervalued even when it is paid and thus counted in GDP.

Another, more important, reason for this paradoxical situation is that we live in capitalist economies in which the market decides the value of goods and services. The crux of the problem is that the market is based on 'one-dollar-one-vote', rather than 'one-person-one-vote', system of decision-making (also see 'Garlic' and 'Lime'). In this system, what determines the price of something is how much people are willing to pay for it, rather than how many people need it. However essential something is for some people's survival, it does not count in the market if those people do not have the money to

---

* In terms of shopping, key workers in the UK were allowed to shop in supermarkets before the opening hours or given priority access to basic food and household items in short supply. In terms of education, they were allowed to send their kids to school even when schools were shut in general.

pay for it. This means a huge undervaluation of those 'essential' goods and services – whether it is basic foodstuffs, healthcare, education or care-home services. At the same time, something will be supplied, however non-essential and irrelevant it may be from a commonsensical point of view, if some people are willing to pay for it. Hence the absurd situation that billionaires had a 'space race' in the middle of a pandemic, during which many healthcare staff were getting sick because they did not have adequate personal protection equipment, Covid-19 patients were dying because of a shortage of medical staff and medical equipment and nursing-home residents were contracting Covid-19 because they could not get proper care.*

Like how the Sichuan restaurant in my story treated chillies, we have come to take the presence of unpaid care work, mostly done by women, for granted, despite the fact that our economy and society cannot exist without it. This sexist bias and the accompanying practice of gender discrimination, when combined with the very way in which the market values things, have resulted in a significant undervaluation of paid care work too. The combination of these two aspects has meant that we are at best grossly underrating and at worst completely ignoring many of the most essential human activities and thus creating a totally biased view of what is important for human welfare.

In order to correct this situation, we need to change our perspectives, practices and institutions regarding care work.[III]

First, perspectives. We need to recognize the importance, or rather the essential nature, of care work, both paid and unpaid, for human survival and welfare. We need to stop thinking that the

---

* Lest the reader form an excessively negative view of the market, let me add that it has its merits. Two of them stand out. First, the market system enables us to aggregate and process a vast amount of information that is necessary in running a complex economy. The failure of socialist central planning attests to this merit. Second, by rewarding those who come up with ideas that serve consumers well, it provides incentives to raise productivity. However, these merits of the market need to be set against its limitations, many of which have been discussed in various chapters in this book.

value of something should be determined by the market. We also need to part with the idea that care work is women's work.

Second, the changes in our perspectives need to be translated into reality through changes in our practices – reducing the gender wage gap,* opening up traditionally male-dominated professions more to women and fighting racial discrimination (so that poorly paid care work does not become the only option for ethnic-minority women).

Third, these changes in perspectives and practices need to be socially cemented by institutional changes.[†] Recognition of unpaid care work should be formalized by changes in the welfare system – granting of longer paid care leave for both genders (childcare, eldercare, care for sick relatives or friends), provision of affordable childcare for both stay-at-home parents and parents in paid employment and the introduction (where it doesn't exist) or strengthening of 'carer credits' in calculating pensions. The recognition of the importance of paid care work should be backed up by the raising of minimum wages and the legal requirements for better working conditions in the care sectors. More broadly, the marketization of care services should be restricted and carefully regulated, so that everyone, regardless of income, has access to basic care services.

---

* The gender wage gap is around 20% on average worldwide, although it could be as high as 45% as in Pakistan or Sierra Leone or as low as zero, as in Thailand, or even negative, as in the Philippines or Panama. The data are from the ILO (International Labour Office), *Understanding the Gender Pay Gap*, June, 2020.
† The importance of institutional change is best illustrated by the treatment of the NHS (National Health Service) workers in the UK. In the early days of the pandemic in 2020, millions of people hailed them as 'heroes' and came out into their gardens and streets at a designated time once a week to clap to thank them. This practice lasted for ten weeks under the name Clap for Our Carers. However, in the March 2021 pay settlement for NHS workers, the UK government offered a 1% rise, which was widely described by NHS workers as a 'slap in the face'. It is a very trite thing to say, but, if you want to make a change permanent, changes in sentiments and individual practices are not enough – 'Claps don't pay the bills', as the slogan of one of the campaigns to improve the pay for NHS workers goes. The change has to be backed up by change in institutions.

Food without chillies is unthinkable for billions of people around the world. Life without care work, whether paid or unpaid, is unthinkable for all humanity. But their very necessity and thus ubiquity make chillies and care activities invisible and thus under-valued – or even unvalued. Duncan's acceptance of the different perspective on chilli held by the Sichuan restaurant in my story, and the change in his eating practice, has opened new food horizon for him and led to a better culinary life. Likewise, we need to change our perspectives, practices and institutions regarding care work if we are to build a better world that is more balanced, more nurturing and fairer.

PART FIVE

Thinking About the Future

14

Lime

Caipirinha/Caipiroska
(Brazilian)
Cachaça/Vodka with lime juice and sugar

The success (from the British point of view, of course) of the British Empire – the largest empire in history by population (531 million in 1938)[112] and by area (34 million km² in 1922)[113] – cannot be explained by a single factor. Britain's industrial supremacy was obviously at the heart of it. Its famed skill for divide-and-rule allowed it to run colonies with small armies (often mostly made up of local mercenaries), making it possible for it to control more than ten times its own population.[114] At the most immediate level, however, it was its ability to control the oceans through superior naval forces, which made such a large and dispersed empire feasible – 'Britannia* rules the waves', as one version of the patriotic song 'Rule Britannia' goes.

From the sixteenth century, Britain started competing with Spain, the Netherlands and then France for European – and eventually global – naval supremacy. Over the next couple of centuries, it edged out its competitors one by one by investing aggressively in the construction of a well-armed, well-provisioned and well-run navy.[115] The Battle of Trafalgar in 1805, in which the Royal Navy, under the command of Admiral Horatio Nelson, defeated the combined fleets of the French and the Spanish navies, sealed Britain's global naval supremacy for more than a century.

With such a strong navy, Britain, given its island status, was

---

* The female warrior in a helmet and with a trident who personifies Britain.

virtually uninvadable. Safety from external invasion, in turn, allowed the country to use its relatively small (and thus economical) army almost exclusively for maintaining internal order, by suppressing the (not infrequent) revolts against its notoriously inegalitarian socio-economic order.[116] Above all, the strong navy enabled it to expand its empire by capturing far-flung lands, repelling attempts of rival powers to take over the captured lands and protecting from piracy its commercial ships engaged in colonial trade.[117]

And in the ascendancy of the British navy, a tiny, cheap fruit called lime played a critical role.

In the early days of European trans-oceanic voyages on sailing ships, which started in the late fifteenth century, the biggest killer of sailors was not enemy ships, not pirates, nor even storms. It was scurvy – a horrible disease whose symptoms included lethargy, swollen and bleeding gums, loose teeth, severe joint pain and often death.

We now know that scurvy is caused by the lack of vitamin C in the body, but its cause remained a mystery until the twentieth century. Unlike most other animals, humans cannot synthesize vitamin C, so they need to take it orally.[118] Subsisting on a diet of rancid salted meat, weevil-infested biscuits ('hard tack') and stale beer for months on end, sailors on trans-oceanic voyages developed scurvy and died off like flies.* Scurvy was so prevalent that ship-owners and governments are said to have assumed a 50% death rate from it for sailors embarking on any major long-distance voyage.[119] It is estimated that scurvy killed more than 2 million sailors worldwide between the time of Columbus's transatlantic voyage and the mid-nineteenth century.[120]

Naturally, there was a frantic search for a cure for scurvy. All sorts of remedies, including vinegar and vitriolic acid, were tried. Slowly, the juice of citrus fruits came to be known as an effective cure,

---

* The human body can store vitamin C for at least for a month and usually up to three months, so scurvy was not a big problem among sailors before their voyages became trans-oceanic.

although until the twentieth century it was not understood that the active ingredient was vitamin C. The search for the cure for scurvy was so important in the discovery of vitamin C that the scientific name for the vitamin is ascorbic acid, which literally means 'anti-scurvy acid'.

The effectiveness of citrus juice against scurvy was also known by its rival navies, but the Royal Navy was the first to apply the solution systematically.[121] In 1795, the Admiralty made lemon juice a compulsory item on a sailor's ration and, cleverly, ensured its consumption by mixing it in the ration of watered-down rum, known as 'grog'. Lemon was soon replaced by lime. This was partly because lime was cheaper and easier to provision – unlike lemons, limes grew in Britain's Caribbean colonies. But it was also because lime was considered more effective, as it was then mistakenly believed that scurvy was cured by acidity (in which lime is higher than lemon) rather than by vitamin C (whose level in lime is only around half that in lemon).

Within just over a decade of the introduction of lemon and then lime juices, scurvy virtually disappeared in the Royal Navy.[122] Consumption of lime became such a prominent feature of the Royal Navy that British sailors came to be called 'limeys' by the Americans – a name that eventually came to mean all Brits in the US.

Another country for which lime is a symbol of national identity is Brazil. Lime is the key ingredient in the country's national alcoholic drink, *caipirinha*. It's made from lime juice (although the juices of other fruits, such as passion fruits, are also used) sugar, and *cachaça*, Brazil's national liquor.*

Cachaça is distilled from fermented sugar cane juice (so *caipirinha* is sugar, sugar and lime!). If distilled to a high degree, sugar cane juice becomes ethanol, which can be used as a fuel for automobiles. As the largest producer of sugar cane in the world, Brazil had

---

* *Caipirinha* can be made with vodka, in which case it is called *caipiroska*. Personally I prefer it, as I find *cachaça* a little too sweet.

experimented with the use of ethanol as a fuel for motor cars since the early twentieth century.* But following the collapse in international trade due to the Great Depression and then the Second World War, which made the importation of oil difficult, its government started seriously pushing for the use of ethanol fuel, by making a 5% mixture of ethanol into gasoline mandatory and subsidizing the ethanol industry. After the Second World War, the use of ethanol declined with cheap oil, but after the first Oil Shock in 1973, the Brazilian government introduced an ambitious programme to promote the substitution of petroleum with ethanol.

Brazil's 1975 National Ethanol Program (Proálcool) subsidized both sugar producers' investments in ethanol production capacity and the price of ethanol at the pump.[123] In the late 1970s, car producers operating in Brazil (such as Fiat and Volkswagen) even developed engines that could exclusively be run on ethanol. By 1985, 96% of all new cars sold in Brazil had all-ethanol engines. Since then, there have been ups and downs for the programme, with fluctuations in oil price, sugar cane production and the scale of government subsidies. But the launch of the 'flexi-fuel' cars, which can run on any mixture of gasoline and ethanol, by Volkswagen in 2003, followed by other manufacturers, has secured ethanol's place as a major energy source for Brazil. Today, ethanol supplies 15% of its annual energy production. No wonder the American historian Jennifer Eaglin titled her important study on the history of ethanol fuel in Brazil 'More Brazilian than *Cachaça*'.[124]

Outside Brazil, ethanol and other modern biofuels (such as biodiesel, made with plant oils like as rapeseed or soybean, or animal fat) have seriously entered the energy system only in the last couple of decades.† With increasing concerns about climate change,

---

* Henry Ford's Model-T, the first mass-produced car, launched in 1908, also ran on a gasoline-ethanol mixture.
† I say 'modern biofuels', because technically speaking firewood or animal dung are also biofuels.

dozens of countries are now requiring the mixing of ethanol in gasoline and biodiesel in diesel oil, in an attempt to reduce the use of fossil fuels.

The world is already experiencing melting polar ice and rising sea levels, increases in the strength and frequency of extreme weather events (heatwaves, cyclones, flooding, wildfire), and mass extinction of species. There is a scientific consensus that, if the rise in global temperature is not controlled very soon by radically reducing the emission of greenhouse gases (such as CO_2, methane, nitrous oxides, etc.), humanity will face an existential threat in the coming decades.

First, we need new technologies. And lots of them.

Above all, we need alternative energy technologies that will enable us to generate energy without emitting greenhouse gases (GHGs) – biofuels, solar power, wind energy, wave power, hydroelectricity, hydrogen fuel and even nuclear power as a stop-gap measure in some circumstances.[125] Capturing emitted carbon and either using or burying it could also play a (minor) role.* We need more effective ways of storing electricity, so that we can use the intermittent electricity generated by solar or wind power on a more constant basis.

It is not just new energy technologies that we need. Fossil fuels are used not just as energy sources but in the making of key materials of our modern, industrial way of life – steel, fertilizer, cement and plastic.[126] So, we need to develop technologies that use as little fossil fuel as possible in making these materials, methods for their more efficient recycling and alternative materials whose production requires less (ideally zero) fossil fuel.

We also need 'adaptation technologies' that help us deal with the consequences of climate change. Given more frequent and severe droughts, we need better techniques for irrigation, water recycling and desalination, while developing crops that are more resistant to

---

* This is known as CCUS, or carbon capture, utilization and storage.

extreme weather events. Improvements in weather forecasting and flood control can help us better cope with storms and cyclones that are happening more often and on a larger scale.

Better technologies are necessary but not enough. We also need changes in the way we live – mainly people in the rich countries and richer people in developing countries.

Even with the use of alternative energies, like biofuels, electric batteries and (hopefully) hydrogen fuel cells, we need to drive less in personal vehicles. This is easier said than done, especially in countries, like the US, where a lot of long-distance driving is inevitable because living spaces are spread out and public transport is poor. In such countries, reduction in the use of personal vehicles will require a major investment in public transport and, in the longer run, a radical reorganization of living spaces through changes in urban planning regulations (more on this later).

Then, we can be much more effective with energy use in living and working spaces. More efficient house insulation (e.g., filling of wall cavities, installation of double- or triple-glazed windows) and the use of heat pumps will reduce energy demand for house heating enormously. We can reduce our electricity use by learning to switch lights off more diligently at home. The same should be done to working spaces – office blocks should be better insulated, and we should leave only a limited amount of lighting on in office blocks outside working hours.

Third, changing our eating habits can have a big impact. Agriculture accounts for a substantial amount of greenhouse gas (GHG) emissions (the estimate varies between 15% and 35%).[127] Eating less meat will contribute greatly to cuts in GHGs. Beef is the most important in this regard – according to a recent estimate, it accounts for 25% of all GHG emissions from agriculture[128] (also see 'Prawn' and 'Beef'). We should also try to eat more seasonally – trying to grow things in greenhouses, even if they are 'local', or shipping (or even flying) non-seasonal food items from far away can create huge carbon footprints. I am not suggesting that we should totally give up on food variety, but those who live in rich countries should reduce their expectations for 'on-demand' food.

All these technological possibilities and possible changes in the way we live, however, will not amount to much without concerted, large-scale public action – by local and national governments, by international organizations, and by nations working together. Market incentives and individual choices are not enough.

In terms of technologies, we need active involvement of the government in promoting 'green' technologies. If left to the market, many of the technologies that we need in order to combat and cope with climate change will simply not be developed. This is not because private sector firms are 'evil' but because they are under constant pressure to deliver short-term results – a tendency that has become even worse under financial deregulation (see 'Spices'). In developing and deploying 'green' technologies, we reap the returns in a matter of decades, if not longer. Private sector firms, however, operate with time horizons of years, if not quarters, and thus are understandably reluctant to invest in developing such technologies.

The myopia of the private sector is why large-scale investments in new technologies and their deployment have historically required strong government action. The prime example in this regard is the developments of information technology and biotechnology, which were initially almost exclusively funded by the US government (through federal 'defence' and 'health' research programmes, respectively – see 'Noodle'), as these technologies were highly risky and had long – very long – horizons for returns. In a number of countries in Europe, China, Brazil as well as in the US, low-carbon energy technologies, such as solar power and wind power, have been developed and deployed on significant scales only thanks to government intervention.[129]

We also need public action to ensure that we develop technologies that help poorer countries advance their economies with minimal GHG emission while dealing with the consequences of climate change. The market is a one-dollar-one-vote, rather than one-person-one-vote system (also see 'Garlic' and 'Chilli'), so, if left alone, investments will flow into technologies that serve those who have more money. This means that there will be relatively little investment in technologies that poorer countries need the most – efficient energy technologies for agricultural and industrial production or 'climate adaptation technologies'. We need public action to support the development of such technologies and their transfers to developing countries (should they have been developed by researchers and firms in rich countries) at subsidized prices, or even for free. Such action is a necessary step to achieving 'climate justice', given that developing countries have contributed little to climate change but are suffering disproportionately from its consequences, with some of them already literally disappearing under rising sea levels.

Individuals can truly change the way they live only when their pro-environmental choices are enabled by government policies.

Sometimes this is because changes in individual behaviour requires upfront investments that are beyond the means of many individuals. Those improvements in home energy-use efficiency through better insulation, double-glazing and heat pumps require big upfront investments that some individuals cannot afford, even though the investments more than pay for themselves in the long run. Government subsidies and loans are needed if these investments are to be made.

Sometimes we need public action because leaving it to individuals to make the 'right' choice in the market to deal with a systemic problem, like climate change, is not only unfair but ineffective. 'Greener eating' is the best example in this regard. In theory, we could require that those who are selling food fully disclose the carbon footprint of their products and let consumers 'shop in the right way' and drive out polluting producers. However, in reality, this is as good as doing nothing. To begin with, consumers do not have the time and the mental capacity to process all the information on the carbon footprints of their food items, even if they are fully disclosed.[130]

Actually it could be worse than doing nothing. Without the government setting the minimum environmental standards, there will be a 'race to the bottom', in which suppliers that pollute more drive out their competitors by offering cheaper products.

Lime may have been an effective antidote to scurvy, but it required executive action by one of the most powerful institutions in the world at the time – the Royal Navy – to use it in an effective way and save sailors' lives in quantity. The Royal Navy did not leave it up to the individual sailor to pack his own citrus before setting sail but mandated its inclusion in the ration and adapted the sailors' favourite tipple (rum) to ensure that vitamin C got to everyone.

So it is with climate change. We know the solutions but, like the Royal Navy and the lime, we cannot leave their implementation to individual choices in the market. We have to use all the mechanisms of collective action at our disposal – local and national governments, international cooperation, and global agreements – to make it sure that those solutions are carried out – food regulations, investments in public transport, changes in urban planning policy, government subsidies for improvements in house insulation, public financing of the development of more energy-efficient technologies and transfer of 'green' technologies to developing countries. The most effective social changes occur when individual change is combined with determined, large-scale public actions.

15

Spices

Monkfish in curried clam broth
(my recipe)
Monkfish (or any firm white fish) served with
curried clam broth

As you'll know by now, I don't have cravings for any particular cuisine – not even Korean. I can happily go without eating Korean food for six months (and I often did when I was a graduate student). Nor do I need to eat Italian, Mexican or Japanese food regularly, even though these are favourites.

There is one exception: 'Indian' food – or rather South Asian food.* If I don't eat South Asian food for a couple of weeks, I miss it.

It's ironic: I disliked South Asian food when I first tried it. With most other new cuisines, it was instant affection. I fell for Thai food head over heels when I first tried it in a Thai restaurant in Soho back in the late 1980s. Greek food – moussaka, taramasalata, loukaniko sausages, you name it – was an instant hit. I didn't even sense I was eating 'foreign' food when I ate in Italy during my first visit there in 1987. But 'Indian'? No.

To my (non-South Asian) friends, I complained that South Asian food lacked 'body'. I don't know exactly what I was trying to say, but I must have been unhappy at a subconscious level about the relative

---

* I am saying 'Indian' in inverted commas, as more than eight out of ten 'Indian' restaurants in the UK are run by people of Bangladeshi origin, 95% of whom are estimated to be from just one province of the country, Sylhet (see A. Gillan, 'From Bangladesh to Brick Lane', *Guardian*, 21 June, 2002). So, I call the cuisine 'South Asian' rather than 'Indian' here and elsewhere in the book.

lack of *umami* flavour – the want of soy sauce and shortage of garlic – in the dishes that I had tried. However, thinking back, I think the real reason for my complaint was that I couldn't handle the complex and unusual sensations that the multitude of spices in South Asian dishes hit me with.

Until I came to Britain, I had known only five spices – black pepper, mustard, cinnamon, ginger and chilli. And of these five, I had seen only cinnamon, ginger and chilli in their raw forms; black pepper was greyish, dusty powder, rather than peppercorns, and mustard came in a preparation similar to that of English mustard (although milder and sweeter in taste).

Sure, I had eaten Chinese 'five-spice (*wuxiang*) pork' a few times. But I wasn't too keen on it and didn't bother to find out what those five spices were (they are star anise, cloves, cinnamon, Sichuan pepper and fennel seeds, in case you are wondering), so it was as good as not having consumed them at all.

Over time, however, I came to appreciate and then fall deeply in love with the complex of flavours, aromas and sensations that the huge gamut of spices give to South Asian dishes – coriander seeds, mustard seeds, cumin, clove, nutmeg, mace (the shell of nutmeg), star anise, fennel seeds, caraway (*jeera*), saffron, cardamom, tamarind, asafoetida and so on.

Today, I am a spice fiend. I make pared-down versions of South Asian dishes, using mainly ground coriander seeds, fennel seeds and cumin, as I find the use of the authentic range of spices a bit daunting and unnecessary (when there is such excellent South Asian food to be had, both from restaurants and in the form of ready-made meals). *Masala chai*, sweet South Asian tea boiled with milk and ginger, cardamom and various other spices, is a favourite drink.

It is not just South Asian dishes for which I use spices. Generous quantities of black pepper, whether in whole corns or in ground form, go into most of the stews and pasta dishes I cook. When I make crumble (apple and rhubarb is my favourite filling, although I also make plain apple crumble and plum crumble), I lace the filling with ridiculous quantities of cloves, cardamom pods and cinnamon (powder or bark). Sometimes I throw in black pepper-corns as well, to increase the heat. I make risotto only with a pinch of saffron – as long as I use a good stock,* it doesn't need anything else. I have recently been totally sold on the South Asian 'cheese toastie' (toasted cheese sandwich for non-Brits – also see 'Anchovy'), with liberal lashings of ground coriander seeds and chilli powder, as well as chopped onion, garlic and coriander leaves (I use the recipe by the British-Indian lawyer-turned-chef Nisha Katona).

Once my conversion to spices happened, I could not believe what I had missed for the first three decades of my life. I cursed my ances-tors. Why didn't they learn to cook with wonderful things like cloves (my favourite!) and coriander seeds? Wouldn't Korean food have been more sophisticated and interesting, had we used star anise and fennel seeds?

Then I realized that I was being unfair. My ancestors were stuck in the north-eastern corner of the Eurasian continent, where it is too cold for most spices to grow. Moreover, unlike the Europeans, they didn't have the willingness (or the ability) to invade and occupy the spice lands.

The spices that have been most prized in Europe – black pepper, clove, cinnamon and nutmeg – used to grow only in what used to be called the 'East Indies', that is, South Asia (especially Sri Lanka and southern India) and South-east Asia (especially Indonesia).[†]

It is well known that the search for spices was a critical impetus behind the discovery of navigational routes from Europe to Asia. Less well known is the fact that it also gave us the most important

---

* My go-to stock recipe consists of chicken carcass, celery, onion, Swiss Marigold vegetarian stock powder and a dash of *myulchi-jut*, the Korean fermented anchovy sauce (see 'Anchovy').

† Given that Columbus and other early European invaders of the Americas thought those lands to be India, it seems that the Europeans thought that all the world except Europe, Africa, the Middle East and China was India.

vehicle for the development of capitalism, namely, the joint stock company, or the limited liability company.

In the beginning, the spice trade with the 'East Indies' was extremely risky for the Europeans. Traversing two, or even three, oceans (the Atlantic, the Indian Ocean and – if you are going to Indonesia – the Pacific) on a sailing ship was like, to exaggerate a bit, sending a Mars probe – and successfully getting it back – these days.[131]

The rewards were fabulous, to be sure, but given the risk involved, investors were reluctant to sink money into the spice race. The risk was further exacerbated by the fact that if a business venture failed the investors could lose everything – not just the money they invested in the venture, but their properties (house, furniture, even pots and pans), as they were expected to repay everything they had borrowed. In more technical terms, their liabilities were unlimited. Failing in a business venture could even cost businessmen their personal freedom. If the creditors remained unpaid even after he had sold everything he owned, the indebted businessman ended up in a debtors' prison.

Potential investors were naturally reluctant to invest in very risky ventures, like the spice trade. A solution was found in offering investors limited liability. Potential investors were given the guarantee that their liability would be limited to what they had invested in the venture (their 'shares'), rather than everything they owned. This hugely reduced the risk that potential investors faced, enabling those who were organizing high-risk ventures to mobilize huge sums of money by recruiting a large number of investors.

So began companies like the English East India Company (founded in 1600) and the Dutch East India Company (1602). They were actually not the first limited liability companies, but their successes in bringing in spice from the East Indies and eventually running colonies in, respectively, India and Indonesia (yes, companies, rather than countries, had colonies in the early days) gave the institution of limited liability a critical boost.

*

Limited liability is the norm today, but until the late nineteenth century, it used to be a privilege granted by the crown – and the government, when absolute monarchy ended – only to high-risk ventures of national importance, like long-distance trade and colonial expansion.

Many were sceptical of the idea, even for such exceptional cases. Among them was Adam Smith, the father of economics, who condemned limited liability companies on the grounds that it let their managers gamble with 'other people's money' (his words). The reasoning was that such managers, who by definition did not own 100% of the companies, would always take excessive risk, because they did not have to bear the full costs of failure.

This is absolutely true, but the point is that limited liability also lets us mobilize capital on a much larger scale than under unlimited liability. This is why Karl Marx, the scourge of capitalism, sang praises of limited liability companies as 'capitalist production in its highest development', although he did so with the ulterior motive that faster development of capitalism would mean faster advent of socialism (as his theory was that socialism will emerge only after capitalism is fully developed).

Soon after Marx made his pronouncement in the mid-nineteenth century, the rise of 'heavy and chemical industries' that require large-scale investments – iron and steel, machines, industrial chemicals, pharmaceuticals and the like – made limited liability even more necessary. You simply cannot get away with issuing permits for limited liability on a case-by-case basis any more, if most of your key industries, and not just long-distance trading or colonial ventures, need large-scale finance. As a result, in the late nineteenth century, most countries made limited liability a right (subject to meeting some minimum standards) rather than a privilege. Since then, limited liability companies (or corporations) have been the main vehicle of capitalist development.

However, this once-mighty vehicle of economic progress has recently been turning into an obstacle to it. Financial deregulation in the last few decades has created so many financial opportunities that share-holders no longer have long-term commitments to companies they legally own. For example, the average period of shareholding in the UK has fallen from five years in the 1960s to less than a year these days. If you cannot commit your money even for a year, can you really say that you share ownership in the company?

In order to keep restless shareholders happy, professional managers have given them an extremely high share of profits in dividends and share buybacks (the practice in which companies buy their own shares and thus raise the share prices, so that shareholders can 'cash in' by selling the shares they own, if they so wish). In the last couple of decades, in the US and the UK, the proportion of corporate profit thus given to shareholders reached 90–95%, when it used to be less than half before the 1980s. And given that retained profit – profit that has not been distributed to shareholders – is the major source of corporate investments, this change has seriously weakened the ability of companies to invest, especially in projects whose returns come in the long run (also see 'Lime').

The time has come to reform the institution of limited liability, so that we retain its benefits while limiting its harmful side-effects.

First of all, limited liability may be modified to encourage long-term shareholding. For example, voting rights can be linked to the length of shareholding period, so that longer-term shareholders have louder voices – this is known as 'tenure voting'. Some countries, such as France and Italy, already practise it, but only in very attenuated forms (shareholders of more than two years getting another vote, that sort of thing). We need to strengthen tenure voting seriously by giving, for example, one extra vote to a share for each additional year owned (perhaps with a ceiling of, say, twenty votes per share). In some way, we need to reward long-term commitment by investors.

Second, we should limit the power of shareholders, even the longstanding ones, by giving a bigger say in company management to other 'stakeholders' – like workers, suppliers of inputs, and local communities where the companies are located. The (strength and) problem with shareholders is that even the longstanding ones can leave any time. By giving some power to stakeholders that are far less mobile than the shareholders, we would allocate power to constituencies that are more concerned with the long-term future of the company than the supposed 'owners' of it – that is, the shareholders.

Last but not least, the options for shareholders need to be limited, in order to make them more interested in the long-term future of the companies whose shares they own. This can be done by tightening financial regulations over the more speculative end of the range of financial products, thereby reducing the chance of making a 'quick buck' and thus increasing the incentive to make a long-term commitment to a company.[132]

Limited liability has been one of the most important instruments that capitalism has ever invented. However, in an age of deregulated finance and impatient shareholders (or, as a more technical term goes, in the age of 'financialization'), it is turning into an obstacle to, rather than a vehicle for, economic progress. We need to reform the institution of limited liability – and those surrounding it, like financial regulation and mechanisms of stakeholder influence.

In the same way in which the same spice may perk up one dish but ruin another, the same institution may function greatly in one context but turn into a great problem in another.

16

Strawberry

Strawberry 'milk'
(recipe by Hee-Jeong, my wife)
Strawberries mashed in milk with added condensed milk

Strawberry is not a berry – according to the scientific definition.* Neither are blackberries or raspberries. Botanically, grape, blackcurrant, banana, cucumber, tomato, aubergine, watermelon and chilli are berries. Don't worry. There are berries that are scientifically berries too – cranberry, blueberry and gooseberry. Still, you wonder why some of the best minds in botany toiled away and (presumably) debated with each other, only to come up with a scientific category called 'berry' when there are so many things that are called berries that are not, and so many things that aren't that are.

Whether or not it is botanically a berry, strawberry is 'the' berry for most people around the globe. In their natural season, the best strawberries are sweet and flavourful enough to be eaten on their own. At other times, they are usually a little too tart. People sweeten them with sugar or (better yet, in my view) condensed milk. The more adventurous eat strawberries with balsamic vinegar or black pepper – or both. When invited to attend a summer garden party in Britain, expect to be served strawberries with cream poured over them (at the risk of losing a few English friends, I must confess that I do not like this combination).

---

* Botanically, a berry is defined as a fleshy fruit without a stone (pit), produced from a single flower containing one ovary. In the case of strawberry, the fruit is developed not from the ovary but the receptacle that holds the ovary. Strawberry belongs to a sub-category of fruit called 'aggregate fruit'.

We make all sorts of nice sweet things with strawberry: cakes, cheesecakes and tarts (I especially love French *tarte aux fraises*). Strawberry, together with vanilla and chocolate, forms the Holy Trinity of ice cream flavours all around the world, although most 'strawberry' ice creams do not have any real strawberry in them. The English are particularly inventive with strawberry-based desserts, such as Eton mess (a mixture of strawberries, crushed meringue and cream, allegedly invented in Eton College, the private school famous for producing the English political elite) and strawberry trifle (mixture of strawberries, custard, sponge-fingers biscuits soaked in sherry, and controversially[133] strawberry-flavoured jelly, topped with a layer of cream).

These days, the seasonality of strawberry is overcome by imports from different climes or cultivation in greenhouses. But until a few decades ago these practices were expensive, so for most people the only way to taste strawberry outside the season was to make it into jam. There are jams made with other fruits (such as raspberry, peach or apricot), but for most people strawberry jam is 'the' jam.

On top of buttered toast is where strawberry jam is most frequently found. But it could go between bready things, as in British jam-and-cheese sandwich, folded French crêpe, or peanut butter and strawberry jam sandwich – my family's variation on the American classic PB&J, or peanut butter and (grape) jelly sandwich (see 'Banana' on jelly). The best use of strawberry jam for me is to put it on top of British scones, together with clotted cream (by the way, I am declaring strict neutrality regarding the Devon–Cornwall war on the order of jam and cream – both ways taste fine to me).* Russians put strawberry jam (and other fruit jams) in their tea, to sweeten it and to counter the tannic taste of tea – quite a clever little idea, although personally I've grown too fond of British tea with milk to have my tea with fruit jam, other than as an occasional diversion.

*

* The Devon way is cream first and the Cornwall way is jam first.

Strawberry is a very labour-intensive crop, especially in terms of harvesting. Unlike fruits such as apples or grapes, strawberries are often hidden among leaves, sometimes deeply, so they require time to locate. They are soft and thus can get easily bruised in the picking process, so the pickers need to be careful, which adds to the time required in harvesting.

In rich countries with high wages, this high labour intensity is a major problem for strawberry producers, as it can make the fruit very expensive. Smaller farms that are easily accessible from main roads may partly meet this challenge by running PYO (pick your own) schemes, where the customers provide their own labour for picking, but this is not a viable solution for most farms. They try to solve the problem of (potentially) high labour cost by hiring cheap immigrant workers.

In California, which is the biggest agricultural state in the US and which produces over 80% of US strawberry output, such cheap labour is mainly supplied by Mexico. Some 70% of agricultural workers in California were born in Mexico, at least half of whom are 'undocumented', meaning that they are working in the US illegally.[134]

These migrant Mexican workers call strawberry *la fruta del diablo*, the fruit of the devil, as strawberry harvesting is one of the lowest-paid, most difficult and thus least desirable farm work in California.[135] The plants are low (4–5 inches tall and growing from beds that are 8–12 inches high), so you have to constantly bend to pick the fruits – doing this for ten to twelve hours each day, weeks on end, 'can cause excruciating pain and lifelong disabilities'.[136] Most of these workers are paid poorly and work under harsh conditions.[137] In the case of undocumented workers, they are paid only around half of what 'legal' workers are paid, and many are exposed to abusive treatment. Employers know that they cannot run to the police.

In the last couple of centuries, agriculture has been mechanized to a very high degree, at least in rich countries with expensive workers – from oxen- or horse-ploughs, hoes and scythes to tractors, combine harvesters and now even drones.* However, harvesting of strawberries has so far resisted mechanization, given the judgement (where the fruit are hidden and whether they are ripe enough to be picked) and the delicacy (given the fruits' easy bruising) involved in the work.

But things are changing. Finally, we are on the cusp of commercializing robots that can pick strawberries (and other difficult-to-pick fruits and vegetables, like raspberries, tomatoes and lettuce). Currently there are several companies developing robot harvesters that can locate, assess the ripeness of strawberries and then pick them without bruising.[138] These robots are as yet not quite as good as humans, but since they are constantly improving, the time will soon come when the final frontier of agricultural automation – strawberry harvesting – is conquered.

It isn't just the strawberry pickers whose jobs are threatened by automation. These days, you cannot read, listen to or watch news media without being told how robots are soon going to replace most human workers and as a result how most people will be left jobless. The fear of a jobless future is particularly heightened by the development in AI (artificial intelligence) technologies, which enable machines to replace the human brain, rather than just human hands and muscles. Symbolic of this global anxiety about automation is an interactive programme called 'Can a robot do your job?', launched by the *Financial Times* in 2017.

Job loss due to automation has been a constant feature of capitalism – at least for the last two and a half centuries (see 'Chocolate').† And indeed those journalists, economists and business

---

* Agricultural machinery, initially horse-powered, started emerging at the turn of the nineteenth century. The combine harvester (combining the reaper and the threshing machine) was invented in the 1880s. Modern tractors using internal combustion engines emerged in the early twentieth century. Drones are these days used for monitoring crop health, livestock and irrigation systems.
† Since Richard Arkwright, the British inventor, developed the first fully automated (cotton textile) spinning mill, powered by water (the 'water frame'), in

pundits who write for the likes of the *Financial Times* have constantly chided blue-collar workers for resisting economic progress when they tried to delay the introduction of labour-saving technologies for fear of job retrenchment. So why are those reporters and commentators suddenly worried about the impact of automation on jobs?

I smell class hypocrisy here. The members of the commentariat class found it easy to condemn technology-resistant blue-collar workers as 'Luddites' – the early nineteenth-century British textile artisans who thought they could save their jobs by smashing the textile machines that were beginning to replace them – when they thought their own jobs were safe from automation. However, now that automation is affecting white-collar professions which they and their friends are the members of – medicine, law, accountancy, finance, teaching and even journalism* – they are belatedly discovering the fear of technology-driven unemployment and, worse, permanent redundancy of their skills.

But we shouldn't be swept up by the new-found panic about automation among the commentariat class. Automation has been with us for the last 250 years, and we've never seen the mass destruction of jobs on the scale that it is predicted for our future. This is because automation does not only destroy jobs, it also creates them.

First of all, automation itself creates new jobs. For example, robots may destroy strawberry-picking jobs, but automation will create demands for robot engineers, workers producing robots and workers producing robot parts. Moreover, automation may reduce labour requirement per unit of output, but it may also increase the overall labour demand (and thus create more jobs) by making the

---

1771 and Oliver Evans, the American engineer, invented the first fully automated industrial process, in the form of a flour mill, in 1785.

* There are already news media using AI to produce simple articles and to edit highlights for sports games. But AI is capable of producing far more sophisticated things than these. For a fine example, see GPT-3 (the name of the AI), 'A robot wrote this entire article. Are you scared yet, human?' in the British newspaper the *Guardian*, 8 September, 2020.

product cheaper and thus increase the demand for it. According to a study by James Bessen, during the nineteenth century in the US, automation eliminated 98% of the weaving labour required to produce a yard of cloth, but the number of weavers actually grew by four times, because the demand for cotton cloth, thanks to the lower price, increased so much.[139]

Then there is indirect job creation from automation. The advent of the computer and the internet may have destroyed many travel agency jobs (as most of us now book our travels online ourselves), but it has also created other jobs in the travel industry – those who are running the booking sites, those who are renting out accommodation through the likes of Airbnb, or the guides for small, specialized tours that get sufficient customers only because they can advertise on the internet. Last but not least, automation increases productivity and thus per capita income, which creates demands for new goods and services that fulfil more diverse and 'higher' needs, which create new jobs – higher education, entertainment, fashion, graphic design or art galleries.

Plus, we can always collectively decide to create more jobs through policy measures. It has been a standard practice at least since the 1930s that, in an economic downturn, when private-sector firms are reducing their spending (by cutting investment or jobs), the government increases its spending and boosts the level of demand in the economy, which then gives the private-sector firms the incentive not to sack workers or even hire new ones. During the Covid-19 pandemic, many rich-country governments went as far as paying a high proportion of the wages of 'redundant' workers to keep them from being sacked (up to 80% in the case of the UK government's 'furlough scheme'). But governments can also create – and have created – jobs through regulations. If a government introduces a regulation demanding a higher number of workers per people served in education (teachers per pupil in schools, nurses per child in nurseries), healthcare (doctors or nurses per patient in hospital), or old people's care (carers per resident in nursing homes), it will create more jobs in those industries. And, as we have seen in the Covid-19 pandemic, these are exactly the sectors which need to hire more people in order to provide good-quality services (see 'Chilli').

With all these forces at play, pulling in different directions, acting in unpredictable ways and unfolding over a long period, it is impossible to say that automation in one particular area – whether it is strawberry harvesting, cotton cloth weaving or journalism – reduces overall employment or not. But the fact that most people have had jobs (however many of them may have been less than ideal, even hazardous or oppressive) throughout 250 years of continuous automation suggests that the overall impact of automation on jobs so far has not been negative.

Some may say it is different this time around, as now machines are replacing workers in jobs that used to be unautomatable. But it is in the nature of technological progress that most people don't see it coming until it arrives. If you told an upper-middle-class British lady in 1900 that most of her maids' work would be done by machines in a couple of generations, she would have laughed in your face. But then came along washing machines, vacuum cleaners, microwave ovens, refrigerators, machines that produced ready-made meals and so on. If you told a Japanese machinist in 1950 that in a few decades most of his work would be done by a machine (lathe) controlled by another machine (a computer), he would have thought you mad. But now CNC (computer numerical control) machines are standard in factories in rich countries.* Fifty years into the future, many people may find it difficult to understand why so many people in the early twenty-first century thought so-called white-collar jobs were unautomatable.

---

* In his prophetic 1951 novel *Player Piano*, Kurt Vonnegut, the American sci-fi writer, depicted a world of unprecedented prosperity, where physical human labour is not needed any more thanks to highly efficient CNC machines. In that world, however, most people – except for a small cadre of managers, engineers and scientists – are miserable, even though they do not lack in material comfort and have loads of leisure time, as they have few useful things to do and, more importantly, feel that they are redundant to society.

All of this does not mean that we can ignore the impact of automation on jobs. It does destroy certain jobs even while creating others, and its impact on those who are made redundant is devastating. Even if the overall impacts of automation on overall employment is not negative in the long run, that is no consolation for those workers who have lost their jobs.

In theory, those who are made redundant due to machines making their skills obsolete can retrain and get another job. This has been the standard assumption among free-market economists, who believe that people are unemployed only because they don't want to work at going wage rates. In reality, without a range of state support, it is very difficult – if not totally impossible – for such workers to get the retraining needed for re-employment, unless they accept low-skilled jobs – stacking shelves in supermarkets, cleaning offices or guarding building sites. Displaced workers need unemployment benefit and income supports that will see them through the retraining process. They need an affordable retraining system, which means government subsidies for the training institutes and/or for the trainees. They need effective (not just cosmetic) help with job search, such as the ones provided through the so-called Active Labour Market Policy in countries like Sweden and Finland.[140]

Automation has come to be seen as 'the' destroyer of jobs when it isn't, in the same way in which strawberry has become 'the' berry despite being a non-berry. We need to see automation for what it is. It is *not* a net destroyer of jobs. Moreover, technology does not fully determine the number of jobs available. Society can act to create new jobs, if it wants – through fiscal policies, through labour market policies and through regulation of certain industries.

Only when we see automation for what it is can we overcome technophobia ('automation is bad') and the sense of hopelessness among the young generation ('we are not going to be needed') that are beginning to haunt the world.

17

Chocolate

Fernanda's brownies
(from Fernanda Reinert, a Norwegian friend)
For the gooiest brownies you'll ever have:
sugar, flour, eggs, baking powder and lots of cocoa powder

I have a confession to make. I am an addict.

My habit started in the mid-1960s, when I was a toddler (yes, I was precocious). The illegal substance that I first got hooked was smuggled out of American military bases and sold in black markets in South Korea of my childhood.

It was called M&Ms.

Black market in M&Ms? I am not making it up. At the time in Korea, the importing of foreign goods other than the machines and the raw materials directly needed for the country's industrialization was banned – passenger cars, TVs, biscuits, chocolates, even bananas, you name it. Smuggling in things like cars and TVs from abroad was very difficult, but enterprising Koreans smuggled smaller consumer items on a large scale out of the American military bases that dotted the country at the time (we still have some). Tinned goods (I remember Dole fruit cocktails and Spam being particularly popular), juice powders (Tang was the thing!), biscuits, chewing gum and chocolates were sold on to itinerant peddlers, who would then sell them to middle-class families with a bit of extra cash to spare.

Chocolates, like M&Ms and Hershey milk chocolate bars, were among the most popular. No one produced chocolate in Korea until 1967, and it wasn't really up to much until 1975, when we got the

Gana chocolate bar, made exclusively with cacao beans imported from Ghana (Korean alphabets cannot spell 'gh' and the 'h' in it is not pronounced anyway) by Lotte confectioner – it is still the country's longest-running brand of chocolate.

Starting from my M&M days, I have spent almost six decades constantly struggling with (and usually giving in to) my desire to consume everything and anything that has to do with cacao beans.

At the top end, there are bars, truffles, florentines and other wonderful things from upmarket chocolatiers, like – in alphabetical order, so that I don't show any favouritism here – Hotel Chocolat (British), Lindt & Sprüngli (Swiss), Pierre Marcolini (Belgian), Republica del Cacao (Ecuadorian) and Valrhona (French). I am not enough of a connoisseur to put much value in the single-estate origin of cacao beans in a chocolate bar or to fuss about the differences in flavour between, say, Venezuelan and Trinidadian beans, that these chocolatiers often highlight, but I cannot resist the intensity and the complexity of flavours and aromas that they are able to conjure.

Liking those very refined chocolate products, however, does not mean that I am a snob. I take chocolate in all its forms.

I often choose regular, dependable chocolate bars, like Cadbury's Dairy Milk or Gana Chocolate bar over 70%-cacao bars or a box of exotic truffles from one of the luxury chocolate-makers. Many of my fellow addicts, especially in Europe, are rather rudely dismissive of Hershey's chocolate bar for not having enough chocolate in it. According to a BBC report, it has only 11% chocolate – less than half that of a chocolate bar that contains so little chocolate that it does not dare call itself 'chocolate', that is, Cadbury's Dairy Milk, with a 23% chocolate content.[141] However, I still have a very soft spot for Hershey's, having acquired the taste for it during my M&M days. And, hey, for me, chocolate is chocolate – whether it is 70%, 23% or 11%.

If you are adding anything to chocolate, I will have to vote for peanuts – just think peanut M&Ms, various Reese's products and – my favourite – Snickers. I would also gladly scoff chocolate-covered whole almonds, break into the sharp peaks of Toblerone bars with their little nut pieces or enjoy the Holy Hazelnut Trinity of Ferrero

Rocher chocolate balls (a whole roasted hazelnut in the centre, hazelnut pieces and hazelnut chocolate). I have mixed feelings about adding fruits to chocolate, but I am partial to orange and chocolate combinations: Terry's Chocolate Orange, dark chocolate-covered candied orange slices, even Jaffa Cakes. Bring them on.

Introduce flour (with fat, especially butter, and sugar) to chocolate and you are creating a whole new universe. Chocolate brownies, chocolate fudge cake, chocolate and Guinness cake, molten 'lava' chocolate cake, Black Forest cake . . . And then all those biscuits and cookies! I like chocolate-biscuit bars like Kit Kat and Twix, but chocolate digestives are my absolute favourite. Then there are all those chocolate chip cookies that I cannot get enough of – Maryland, Pepperidge Farm, supermarket own-brand ones and home-baked ones.

Last but not least, there are non-confectionery modes of chocolate consumption. When I was a kid, I loved drinking chocolate (*kokoa*, as we called it in Korea then), although these days I drink it rarely, having moved on to tea and coffee. I don't generally like ice cream very much, but if it's got chocolate in it in any form, I will gladly eat it. I sometimes sprinkle cacao nibs over breakfast cereals, yoghurt or ice cream. A friend recently taught me to add a couple of squares of a dark chocolate bar when making *chilli con carne*, which works wonders. When I go to Mexico, I often try chicken with *mole poblano*, a sauce made with chocolate and chilli.

I could go on. But you get the picture.

Chocolate is made from the seeds of the cacao tree (*Theobroma cacao*). It originates in Meso-America, although these days its main producers are actually outside the region – Côte d'Ivoire, Ghana and Indonesia being the three largest producers. There is a debate about it, but it is believed that the cacao tree was first domesticated in modern-day Ecuador and Peru. It was enthusiastically adopted by the nations of modern-day Mexico – the Olmecs, the Mayans and the Aztecs. Aztecs were super-keen on the cacao 'beans' (which are of course not beans but the seeds of the cacao fruit, or cacao pod), making a cold drink of chocolate mixed with corn purée and laced with chilli, allspice, and vanilla. Because cacao tree cannot grow in the highlands that are home to the Aztecs, cacao beans were particularly valued by them. The Mayans and the Aztecs are said to have used the cacao bean as a form of currency.

The Spaniards brought chocolate back home from Mexico in the sixteenth century after their conquest of the Aztec empire, which is why the current names of the substance derive from the Aztec word, *xocolātl*.

When it was first brought to Europe, chocolate was a drink – in the original Aztec fashion. By that time, however, the Spaniards in Mexico had taken the chilli out (wimps!) and added sugar or honey to the original Aztec recipe. (Drinking) chocolate started to spread rapidly throughout Europe from the seventeenth century.

Chocolate was made solid only in 1847. Fry's of Bristol, one of the then triumvirate of British Quaker confectioners (together with Cadbury's of Birmingham and Rowntree's of York), invented the first mass-produced chocolate bar.

Though the practice of mixing chocolate drinks with milk had been around for a couple of centuries, the initial chocolate bar was made of dark – rather than milk – chocolate. This is not because dark chocolate was more popular than milk chocolate. It was because all the earlier attempts to add milk to chocolate bars had failed because of the resulting excess liquid, which allowed mildew to develop.

This problem was solved in 1875 by two Swiss. Daniel Peter, a chocolatier, created the first milk chocolate bars by ditching fresh milk and using powdered milk, invented by Henri Nestlé, the wizard of milk-based processed food technology. The two later joined forces with others to form the food giant Nestlé. In 1879, Lindt & Sprüngli, another Swiss firm, made the next leap in chocolate making by inventing the process of 'conching', which improved the texture and the flavour of chocolate by prolonged machine mixing of ingredients. Switzerland became a byword for high-quality chocolate.

*

Many people think that chocolate is the only thing that Switzerland makes – except for those ludicrously expensive watches that only oligarchs, bankers and sports stars can afford. The widespread view is that it is a country that manufactures few things and lives on services.

A negative spin on this would be that Switzerland is a country that makes a living by taking care of the black money deposited by Third World dictators in its secretive banks and selling tacky souvenirs, like cuckoo clocks and cow bells (which these days are probably all made in China anyway), to unsuspecting American and Japanese tourists. A positive – and more prevalent – spin is that the country is a model for the post-industrial economy, in which prosperity is based on services, like finance and high-end tourism, rather than manufacturing.

The discourse of the post-industrial age, originating from the 1970s, starts from the simple but powerful idea that people increasingly want finer things as they become richer. Once people fill their bellies, agriculture declines. When they meet other more basic needs, like clothing and furniture, they move on to more sophisticated consumer goods, like electronics and cars. When most people have these things, consumer demand shifts to services – eating out, theatre, tourism, financial services and so on. At that point, industry begins to decline, and services become the dominant economic sector, starting the post-industrial age of human economic progress.

This view of the post-industrial age gained traction in the 1990s, when almost all rich economies started seeing the importance of manufacturing fall and the importance of services rise, both in terms of output and employment – this process is known as 'deindustrialization'. Especially with China emerging as the biggest industrial nation in the world, the proponents of the post-industrial society argued that manufacturing had become what low-technology, low-wage countries like China did, while high-end services, like finance, IT services and business consulting, were the future, especially for rich countries.

And in this discourse, Switzerland, sometimes together with

Singapore, has been touted as the proof that countries can maintain a very high standard of living by specializing in services. Persuaded by the argument and inspired by the examples of Switzerland and Singapore, some developing countries, such as India and Rwanda, even have been trying to more or less skip industrialization altogether and develop their economies by becoming specialized exporters of high-end services.

Unfortunately for the advocates of post-industrial society, Switzerland is actually the most industrialized economy in the world, producing the largest amount of manufacturing output per person.[142] We don't see many 'Made in Switzerland' products partly because the country is small (only around 9 million people) but also because it specializes in what economists call 'producer goods' – machines, precision equipment and industrial chemicals – that ordinary consumers, like you and me, do not see. It is interesting to note that Singapore, another supposed post-industrial success story, is the world's second most industrialized economy. Using Switzerland and Singapore as models of post-industrial service economy is like – how shall I put it? – using Norway and Finland to promote beach holidays.

The advocates of post-industrialism fundamentally misunderstand the nature of recent economic changes. What is driving deindustrialization is mainly changes in productivity, not changes in demand.

This point is easier to see in relation to employment. Because the manufacturing process has become increasingly mechanized, we don't need the same number of workers to produce the same amount of manufacturing output (see 'Strawberry'). With the help of machines and even industrial robots, workers today can produce many multiples of what their parents' generation could. A half century ago, manufacturing took up around 40% of the workforce in the rich countries, but today the same – and sometimes even greater – amount of output is produced with 10–20% of the workforce.

The dynamics of output are a little more complicated. It is true that the importance of manufacturing in the national economy has declined while that of services has risen in these countries. However, this has happened *not* because the demand for services has increased more than has the demand for manufactured goods in absolute terms, as the proponents of the post-industrial discourse would have us believe. It has happened mainly because services are becoming relatively more expensive, given the faster productivity growth in manufacturing than in services. Just think how computers and mobile phones have become so much cheaper over the last couple of decades, compared to haircuts or eating out. If we take into account the effects of such relative price changes, the share of manufacturing in national output has declined only marginally in most rich countries (the UK is an exception) and even increased in some countries (such as Switzerland, Sweden and Finland) in the last few decades.[143]

Contrary to the myth of post-industrialism, the ability to produce manufactured goods competitively remains the most important determinant of a country's living standards (also see 'Anchovy').

Many of the high-productivity services that are supposed to be replacing manufacturing – such as finance, transport and business services (e.g., management consulting, engineering, design) – cannot exist without the manufacturing sector, because it is their main customer. These services look 'new' only because they used to be provided in-house by manufacturing companies (and thus counted as output of the manufacturing sector) but are now supplied by firms specializing in those services (and thus counted as outputs of the service sector).* This is why countries with strong manufacturing industries, like Switzerland and Singapore, also have strong service industries (although the reverse is not necessarily true).

Moreover, manufacturing is still the main source of technological innovation. Even in the US and the UK, where manufacturing accounts for only around 10% of economic output, 60–70% of R&D

---

* Some even argue that these services should be classified as manufacturing activities, rather than services, for this reason. I thank Jostein Hauge for highlighting this point.

(Research and Development) is conducted by the manufacturing sector. The figure is 80–90% in more manufacturing-oriented economies like Germany or South Korea.

The belief that we now live in an age of post-industrial economy has been particularly harmful for the US and the UK. Since the 1980s, these countries, especially the UK, have neglected their manufacturing sector under the illusion that their decline is a positive sign that their national economies are making a transition from an industrial economy to a post-industrial economy. This gave policy-makers a convenient excuse for not doing anything about the decline of the manufacturing sector.

Instead, in the last few decades, the UK and US economies have been driven by over-development of the financial sector, which came crashing down in the 2008 global financial crisis. Since then, the feeble recovery they have generated (economists have been talking about 'secular stagnation' . . .) is based on another financial (and real estate) bubble – through historically low interest rates* and the so-called 'quantitative easing' programme led by the central banks.

The Covid-19 pandemic of 2020–22 revealed that the US and the UK now have financial markets that have nothing to do with the real economy. During the pandemic, stock markets in those countries have gone up to historical heights while the real economy tanked and ordinary people suffered from unemployment and cuts in income – in American parlance, Wall Street and Main Street have nothing to do with each other any more.

Even if the only 'Made in Switzerland' item you have actually bought is chocolate (highly likely unless you live in Switzerland), don't let that fool you. The secret of Swiss success is the world's strongest manufacturing sector, and not things like banking and upmarket tourism, as we commonly think. Indeed, even the Swiss reputation in the field of chocolate originates from the ingenuity of

---

* In the UK, interest rates have never been lower since records began in 1694, with the establishment of the Bank of England.

its manufacturing sector (the invention of powdered milk, creation of milk chocolate and the development of conching technology). It is not due to its competence in the service industries – say, the ability of its banks to come up with sophisticated instalment payment plans for the buyers of chocolate bars or the ability of its advertising agencies to do a sleek marketing campaign for chocolate.

The discourse of post-industrial society, for which Switzerland has been an unwitting role model, is at best misleading and at worst harmful for the real economy. We believe in it at our peril.

Conclusion: How to Eat (Economics) Better

I know. This has been a strange book.

I have talked about dozens of food items, including some that many of you would have never thought of eating – acorn, silkworm pupa, grasshopper and (depending on who you are) garlic and chilli. I have discussed their biological qualities and lineages, geographical origins and spread, the economic and social histories behind them, their political symbolism and often my own personal relationship with (sometimes addiction to) them. I've described numerous ways in which they could be cooked – fried, stewed, flame-grilled, smoke-grilled, baked, roasted and boiled – or not – served raw, salted, pickled or fermented – for eating. I have described and compared different culinary traditions, with their universal appeals, idiosyncrasies and fusions.

In doing so, we have travelled to many different places and different times. In 'Acorn', we went from the mountain tops of contemporary Korea, through the alleys of Inquisition Spain, to the studies of Baghdadi scientists in the eleventh century, then to early twentieth-century Japanese factories, and finally back to today's Korean bank branches. In 'Okra', the journey took us on slave ships on the Atlantic, touched on the slave-based sugar plantations of St Domingue (today's Haiti), encountered the settler farmers of the American prairie, witnessed the violent persecution of Native Americans and cowered in the streets of Santiago under the military dictatorship of General Pinochet.

These food journeys have sometimes led to somewhat predictable economic destinations – it is not too difficult to imagine how one could go from anchovy to the perils of dependence on primary commodities or from strawberry to the impact of automation on jobs. But very often the economic topic and the route through which we arrived was, frankly, bizarre.* I guess only my weird mind could have kicked off with a biting footballer and blown the whistle on the World Trade Organization (WTO) or started talking about scurvy and somehow ended up with a discussion of the economics of climate change.

Through this 'travel' down the rabbit hole', I hope that you have formed your own ideas as to how to 'eat' economics better in the future. When it comes to food, we all work out our own ways to source ingredients (often with constrained budgets), combine and cook them and come up with new ideas (whether it is tweaking your mother's recipe or adapting some dish that you came across on Instagram). It should be the same with economics. You don't need other people to tell you how to learn, critically reflect upon, and use economics. You are all perfectly capable of figuring it out for yourself.

However, as someone who has studied and practised economics for four decades, I think I can offer a few pieces of dietary advice.

First, a varied diet is important. In the book, I have tried to present different perspectives in economics. Often they have different opinions about the same thing (on, say, inequality, as seen in 'Chicken'). Sometimes one perspective lets you see things that others are blind to (for example, the feminist perspective on care work, as highlighted in 'Chilli'). At other times, different perspectives are complementary to each other (as in the case of positive and negative perspectives on multinational corporations, as discussed in 'Banana'). Appreciating different perspectives in economics, like eating a range of different food items and different types of cuisine, makes your economic diet not only richer but more balanced and healthier.

Second, you should be open-minded about trying new things.

---

* And, I admit, following my own idiosyncratic stream of consciousness, although I would like to think that it has been done in a way that does not do disservice to the genre, in which Alan Bennett and W. G. Sebald are the masters.

I've overcome my preconception that a carrot is purely an ingredient for savoury dishes and come to love carrot cake. Conversely, even if you have only known the tomato as a savoury ingredient – in pasta sauces, in salads, in stews – you should try at least once to eat it as a 'fruit' (it *is*, after all, a fruit), dipped in sugar, as Koreans do (see 'Carrot'). Really, if the Brits, once the world champions of food conservatism, can become some of the most open-minded eaters in the world (see 'Garlic'), you can do the same with economics. Even just to know your pet economic theories better and fully understand their strengths and weaknesses, you should learn about other economic theories.

Third, as many of us do with food, you should check the provenance of the 'ingredients' that you are using to 'cook' with. Even though most professional economists would like the rest of the world to believe that what they practise is a science, like physics or chemistry, based on indisputable assumptions and objective facts, economic analyses are often based on myths, 'facts' that are technically correct but misleadingly formulated, or taken-for-granted assumptions that are questionable or even blatantly wrong. When the analysis is based on such low-quality ingredients, the resulting economic 'dish' is at best devoid of nutrients and at worst harmful.

The best example of myth in economics is the distorted historiography that tells us that Britain and then the US became the world's economic hegemons because of their free-trade, free-market policies – when they were the countries that most aggressively used protectionism in order to develop their national industries (see 'Prawn' and 'Beef'). The exclusion of unpaid care work from GDP is an example that shows that even 'factual' things like output statistics can lead to misleading conclusions if they capture only part of the reality or capture it in a biased way (see 'Chilli'). A good example of the last category would be the common assumption that poor countries are poor because their people don't work hard, which diverts our attention from analysing and reforming the structural factors that make those people poor (see 'Coconut').

So, you need to be diligent in 'fact-checking' and, more importantly, in finding out on what theoretical bases the 'facts' have been created. If you use falsehood and biased representation of reality in your economic analysis, you cannot get good results, however good your economic theory may be. Garbage in, garbage out, as they say in America.

Fourth, you should use your imagination. The best cooks (and I don't just mean famous chefs) are people who have rich imaginations. They are the ones who are able to see that some 'sacred' ingredients should be ditched to improve – or even reinvent – a well-known dish. These cooks bring back forgotten ingredients and repurpose well-known ones. They do not get swept up in some food craze, although they understand why it exists and what to learn from it. Good cooks, above all, have the imagination to defy culinary conventions and combine different culinary traditions.

Likewise, good economists – and I don't mean just academic economists but policy-makers, social activists and informed citizens – are those who can do the economic equivalent of 'imaginative' cooking. They are people who can ditch sacred ingredients (such as 'economic freedom' – see 'Okra' and 'Beef'), repurpose existing ingredients (think what the social democrats have done with the 'anti-socialist' welfare state – see 'Rye'), and revive forgotten ingredients (as we could do with the prize system for invention – see 'Carrot'). They are the ones that are not swayed by fads while being able to understand why such fads exist and what we can learn from them (like the ideas of jobless future or post-industrial knowledge economy – see 'Strawberry' and 'Chocolate', respectively). Moreover, the best economists should be, like the best of the cooks, able to combine different theories to have a more balanced view. They understand both the power and the limitations of the market (see 'Lime' and 'Coca-Cola', among others), while knowing that entrepreneurs are the most successful when supported and suitably regulated by the state (see 'Noodle' and 'Spices'). They should be willing to combine individualist theories and socialist (or, more broadly, collectivist) theories – and augment them with theories of human capabilities – in order to come up with a more rounded view on issues like inequality (see 'Chicken'), care work (see 'Chilli') and the welfare state (see 'Rye').

We must all find our own ways to understand (and change) our economy and, with it, the world in which we live and share, in the same way in which we all have to figure out our own ways to eat better – for our own individual health and wallets, for those who are producing food, for those who are not eating enough and / or nutritiously, and, increasingly, for the planet.

Acknowledgements

This book has a long and convoluted history. I had the idea of using food stories to talk about economics soon after I finished writing my first non-academic book, *Bad Samaritans*, back in 2006. It looked like a good way of drawing in readers who don't normally think about economics while giving me an excuse to talk about two of my biggest passions – economics and food – at the same time. I cannot remember exactly when, but sometime in 2007 I sketched out the idea of the book and wrote two sample chapters – 'Acorn' and 'Anchovy'.

Events kept intervening, however. The outbreak of the 2008 global financial crisis prompted me to write a book that more directly dealt with current economic issues, which became *23 Things They Don't Tell You About Capitalism*, published in 2010. After that book, I was ready to restart 'the food book', as I had been calling it, but then I was given an 'offer that I could not refuse' in the form of the invitation to write the very first volume in the relaunched Pelican paperback series by Penguin Books.

After that book came out as *Economics: The User's Guide* in 2014, I was raring to advance 'the food book', when, in 2015, the *Weekend Magazine* team of the *Financial Times* agreed to run several essays of mine on food and economics under the series title 'Thought for Food'. I was given only 700 words per essay, but it gave me the opportunity to produce shorter, more honed versions of 'Acorn' and 'Anchovy', as well as writing what eventually became the seeds of some of the chapters in this book – 'Carrot', 'Chicken', 'Prawn', 'Coca-Cola', 'Chocolate' and 'Spices'. I thank Caroline Daniel, the editor of the *Weekend Magazine*, and her colleagues Isabel Berwick, Sue Matthias and Natalie Whittle for their support for and feedback on my articles.

Even with this opportune springboard, I was still not able to launch 'the food book', because soon after that I got very busy with other things, especially an administrative role in the university I took on. By the end of the 2010s, well over a decade after the idea of the book first came to me, it looked as if it would become one of those books that writers always talk about writing but never do.

I couldn't let that happen, so finally in 2020 I bit the bullet and started working with my literary agent and friend Ivan Mulcahy to make the book 'happen'. Ivan had been discussing the idea of the book with me since its inception back in 2007 but, once I got serious about writing it, he gave me a push to create a clear conceptual framework for the book, without which, I realized, it could easily degenerate into a 'dog's breakfast' of a book. 'Garlic' (I mean the chapter, not the bulb) was born in the process, and from then on the book really came together. I thank Ivan for persuading me to conceptualize the book more clearly and also for helping me sharpen my writing and improve the quality of the arguments.

When a book has a long history of gestation, like this one, it ends up creating *Groundhog Day* experiences for some close friends – the same guy talking about the same book over and over for more than a decade. Jonathan Aldred, Aditya Chakrabortty, Chris Cramer, Jonathan Di John, Felix Martin and Deepak Nayyar are the most prominent members of that unlucky group of friends. All of them have not only patiently listened to my musings and rants about the book but also, over the years, read several chapters in various forms and given me crucial feedback. Duncan Green deserves a special mention. He has discussed the book with me right from when it was no more than a two-page sketch and a couple of very rough draft chapters. Over the years, he read many versions of different chapters and even graciously agreed to appear as the lead character in one of the chapters.

Once the writing got going, I was hugely helped by my editors – Laura Stickney (who was also my editor for *Economics: The User's Guide*) at Penguin Random House and Clive Priddle at Public Affairs. They not only gave me a lot of important comments on substantive and editorial issues but helped me shape the book in a much more exciting and innovative way than I had initially envisaged.

In the process of writing the book, I benefited greatly from inputs from friends. Bob Rowthorn, who had formed me as an economist when he supervised me for my PhD, read the whole manuscript and gave me helpful and encouraging comments. Federico Benninghoff and Helena Perez Niño read all the chapters and shared their erudition and economic logic to help me enrich my arguments. Pedro Mendes Loureiro read almost all the chapters and pushed me to sharpen my arguments. Jostein Hauge and João Silva also provided very helpful comments on all the chapters. Mateus Labrunie and Andy Robinson read many chapters and gave me helpful comments, both on economics and on the food front.

Baptiste Albertone, Fadi Amer, Antonio Andreoni, Jimmy Chan, Hasok Chang, Reda Cherif, Silvana Da Paula, Gary Dymski, Terry Fry, Fuad Hasanov, Amy Klatzkin, John Lanchester, Amir Lebdioui, Jungeun Lee, Connor Muesen, David Pilling, Nicolas Pons-Vignon, James Putzel and Sebastián Torres read various chapters and gave me very useful comments.

Over the years, a number of young people have done background research for the book, without which it would have been much poorer, both in terms of its economics and in terms of its food stories. Marit Andreassen and Anna Rimmer deserve a special mention in this regard for their sterling work. I also thank Baptiste Albertone, Jin-Gyu Chang, Mateus Labrunie, and Nick Testa for their efficient and intelligent research assistance.

Our food experiences are most importantly shaped by our families. I thank my parents for teaching me what good food is and how important it is for our well-being and social bonds. My mother has cooked countless tasty meals, while my father has taken me and my siblings, and later my wife and my children, to eat out in so many good restaurants. I thank my mother-in-law for receiving me into her food world, which is rather different from my mother's, she being from Jeolla-do, south-western Korea, where food is famously varied and complex, and my mother being from what is now North Korea, where food is more down-to-earth and heartier. My father-in-law, whose passing in the early days of writing this book has been the saddest event in my life, was a food connoisseur, who generously shared many excellent dining experiences with me, my wife and my children.

Hee-Jeong, my wife, Yuna, my daughter, and Jin-Gyu, my son, have spent the last fifteen years with this book, on and off. They bought, ate, cooked and talked about many of the food items and dishes in the book with me. In the process, they, sometimes unwittingly, inspired me to develop and polish the food stories in the book. Over the years, they have been the first port of call, and often teachers, for many of my ideas in all sorts of areas – economics, history, environment and science. They read all the chapters and gave me very helpful feedback. Hee-Jeong especially read and discussed with me multiple versions of all the chapters as they were being written, while helping me survive difficult patches in the writing process. I am particularly thankful to her for pushing me to write a chapter on care work ('Chilli'), a topic whose importance I have always recognized but which I felt under-qualified to write about. Doing the research on the topic and writing the chapter has taught me a lot. I dedicate the book to her, Yuna and Jin-Gyu.

Ha-Joon Chang
March 2022

Notes

1 The data are from the Ministry of Agriculture, Food and Rural Affairs of the Republic of Korea (South Korea).

2 http://library.mafra.go.kr/skyblueimage/27470.pdf, p. 347.

3 ISMEA (Institute of Services for the Agricultural Food Market), Il Mercarto dell'aglio, p. 9, http://www.ismeamercati.it/flex/cm/pages/ServeBLOB.php/L/IT/IDPagina/3977.

4 FranceAgriMer, the National Institute of Agricultural Products and Sea Products, https://rnm.franceagrimer.fr/bilan_campagne?ail.

5 Other Spanish pigs are not so lucky. Most pigs in Spain these days are raised in crammed factory farms, fed on processed soybeans. See https://www.lavanguardia.com/internacional/20201224/6143002/navidad-soja-pavo-embutido-procedencia-amazonia.html. I thank Andy Robinson for drawing my attention to this.

6 D. Gade, 'Hogs (Pigs)', in K. Kiple and K. Ornelas (eds.), *The Cambridge World History of Food* (Cambridge: Cambridge University Press, 2000), pp. 539–40.

7 C. Roden, *The Book of Jewish Food – An Odyssey from Samarkand and Vilna to the Present Day* (London: Penguin Books, 1996), pp. 190–91.

8 The quote is from *Japan Times*, 18 August, 1915.

9 B. Webb, *The Diary of Beatrice Webb: The Power to Alter Things*, vol. 3, edited by N. MacKenzie and J. MacKenzie (London: Virago/LSE, 1984), p. 160.

10 S. Webb and B. Webb, *The Letters of Sidney and Beatrice Webb*, edited by N. MacKenzie and J. MacKenzie (Cambridge: Cambridge University Press, 1978), p. 375.

11 The literacy rate data for Korea is from N. McGinn et al., *Education and Development in Korea* (Cambridge, Mass.: Harvard University Press, 1980), table 17. The figures for Thailand, the Philippines and Malaysia are from UNESCO *Statistical Yearbooks*.

12 https://data.oecd.org/hha/household-savings.htm.

13 On the debate on the origin of okra, see C. Smith, *The Whole Okra – A Seed to Stem Celebration* (White River Junction, Vermont: Chelsea Green Publishing, 2019), ch. 1.

14 J. Carney and R. Rosomoff, *In the Shadow of Slavery – Africa's Botanical Legacy in the Atlantic World* (Berkeley: University of California Press, 2009).

15 R. Lipsey, 'U.S. Foreign Trade and the Balance of Payments, 1800–1913', Working Paper no. 4710, NBER (National Bureau of Economic Research), Cambridge, Mass., 1994, p. 22, table 10.

16 M. Desmond, 'In Order to Understand the Brutality of American Capitalism, You Have to Start on the Plantation', *New York Times*, 14 August 2019, https://www.nytimes.com/interactive/2019/08/14/magazine/slavery-capitalism.html. Pedro Mendes Loureiro, my Brazilian economist friend, has told me that the same happened in Brazil, the other main slave economy of the time.

17 K. G. Muhammad, 'The Sugar That Saturates the American Diet Has a Barbaric History as the "White Gold" That Fueled Slavery', *New York Times*, 14 August, 2019, https://www.nytimes.com/interactive/2019/08/14/magazine/sugar-slave-trade-slavery.html.

18 Heart of palm 'has been called "millionaire's salad" on the assumption that the only the very rich can afford to fell an entire palm and have the leaf stalks cut away to expose the large bud, which is the part that is eaten', according to H. Harries, 'Coconut', in Kiple and Ornelas (eds.), *The Cambridge World History of Food*, p. 389.

19 On the use of coconut oil in fish-and-chip shops, ibid. p. 390. On the Jewish origin of fish and chips, see D. Jurafsky, *The Language of Food* (New York: W. W. Norton & Company, 2014), ch. 3, 'From Sikbāj to Fish and Chips'.

20 It is sometimes expanded into a two-commodity economy with coconut and fish – at least they've got the fish part right. See the 'Robinson Crusoe Economy' models in https://en.wikipedia.org/wiki/Robinson_Crusoe_economy.

21 The country data can be found at the World Bank data site at https://data.worldbank.org/indicator/SL.TLF.ACTI.ZS.

22 It was 42% in Burkina Faso, 41% in Benin, 39% in Cameroon, Chad and Sierra Leone. See https://data.unicef.org/topic/child-protection/child-labour/.

23 In 2017, yearly working hours were 2,455 in Cambodia, 2,232 in Bangladesh, 2,209 in South Africa and 2,024 in Indonesia. In the same year, they were 1,354 in Germany, 1,400 in Denmark, 1,514 in France, 1,738 in Japan and 1,757 in the US. See https://ourworldindata.org/working-hours.

24 See H.-J. Chang, *23 Things They Don't Tell You about Capitalism* (London: Penguin Press, 2010), Thing 3, 'Most people in rich countries are paid more than they should be'.

25 S. Collier and W. Sater, *A History of Chile, 1808–2002*, 2nd edition (Cambridge: Cambridge University Press, 2004).

26 A. Doyle, 'Mangroves Under Threat from Shrimp Farms: U.N.', Reuters.com, 14 November 2012, https://www.reuters.com/article/us-mangroves/mangroves-under-threat-from-shrimp-farms-u-n-id USBRE8AD1EG20121114.

27 S. Hussain and R. Badola, 'Valuing Mangrove Benefits', *Wetlands Ecology and Management*, 2010, vol. 18, pp. 321–31.

28 Z. Wood, 'Insects Tipped to Rival Sushi as Fashionable Food of the Future', *Guardian*, 25 June 2019, https://www.theguardian.com/business/2019/jun/25/insects-tipped-rival-sushi-fashionable-food-of-future. For pork, the corresponding figures are 1.1kg and 5kg. The greenhouse gas figure for chicken is not available, but 1kg of live chicken requires 2.5kg of feed.

29 Insects require 23 litres of water and 18m^2 of land per gram of protein produced, in contrast to 112 litres and 254m^2 for beef. For pork, the corresponding figures are 57 litres and 63m^2, while the figures for chicken are 34 litres and 51m^2. See ibid.

30 Ibid.

31 However, Jefferson eventually came around to Hamilton's view, although by that time Hamilton had been long dead (he was killed in 1804 in a pistol duel with Aaron Burr, who was then serving as the vice president under Jefferson). In a letter to Benjamin Austin in 1816, Jefferson said: 'You tell me I am quoted by those who wish to

continue our dependence [sic] on England for manufactures. There was a time when I might have been so quoted with more candor, but within the 30 years which have since elapsed, how are circumstances changed! . . . [E]xperience has taught me that manufactures are now as necessary to our independance [sic] as to our comfort: and if those who quote me as of a different opinion will keep pace with me in purchasing nothing foreign where an equivalent of domestic fabric can be obtained, without regard to difference of price, it will not be our fault if we do not soon have a supply at home equal to our demand, and wrest that weapon of distress from the hand which has wielded it.' See https://founders.archives.gov/documents/Jefferson/03-09-02-0213#X50DC34AA-636D-4AC2-9AA0-91032A2AA417.

32 https://instantnoodles.org/en/noodles/report.html.
33 According to *Hankook Kyungje Shinmoon (Korean Economic Daily)*, https://www.hankyung.com/news/article/2013041875301 (in Korean). Given that the country has 51 million people, this works out to be eleven servings of *chajang-myun* per person per year. Add to this the instant noodle consumption, it works out to be about ninety servings of alkaline noodles per person per year.
34 According to Giugiaro himself in a 1991 interview. See https://jalopnik.com/this-pasta-was-designed-by-the-man-who-designed-the-del-5594815.
35 https://bravearchitecture.com/praxis/giorgetto-giugiaros-inventive-marille-pasta/.
36 https://jalopnik.com/this-pasta-was-designed-by-the-man-who-designed-the-del-5594815.
37 http://www.autotribune.co.kr/news/articleView.html?idxno=2505 (in Korean); and https://oldcar-korea.tistory.com/61 (in Korean).
38 GM produced 4.78 million cars in that year, across its five main brands – in descending order of number of cars produced, Chevrolet (producing around 2.1 million cars a year), Pontiac, Buick, Oldsmobile and Cadillac. Ford produced 1.86 million cars in 1976. See https://en.wikipedia.org/wiki/U.S._Automobile_Production_Figures.
39 https://en.wikipedia.org/wiki/List_of_manufacturers_by_motor_

vehicle_production. The original data are from the International Organization of Motor Vehicle Manufacturers (OICA).

40 In 1976, South Korea's per capita income was $834 in current US dollars. In the same year, Ecuador's was $1,264. Mexico's per capita income was $1,453. The data are from the World Bank, https://data.worldbank.org/indicator/NY.GDP.PCAP.CD.

41 Further information on US protectionism before the Second World War can be found in H.-J. Chang, *Kicking Away the Ladder* (London: Anthem Press, 2002), ch. 2; and H.-J. Chang, *Bad Samaritans* (London: Random House, 2007), ch. 2.

42 For further details on the role of US government in the development of foundational technologies of the information age, see F. Block, 'Swimming Against the Current: The Rise of a Hidden Developmental State in the United States', *Politics and Society*, vol. 36, no. 2 (2008); M. Mazzucato, *The Entrepreneurial State – Debunking Public vs. Private Sector Myths* (London: Anthem Press, 2013); L. Weiss, *America Inc.?: Innovation and Enterprise in the National Security State* (Ithaca, New York: Cornell University Press, 2014).

43 For stories on the origins of orange carrots, see http://www.carrotmuseum.co.uk/history.html, https://www.economist.com/the-economist-explains/2018/09/26/how-did-carrots-become-orange, and https://www.washingtonpost.com/blogs/ezra-klein/post/carrots-are-orange-for-an-entirely-political-reason/2011/09/09/gIQAfayiFK_blog.html.

44 A. Dubock, 'Golden Rice: To Combat Vitamin A Deficiency for Public Health', https://www.intechopen.com/books/vitamin-a/golden-rice-to-combat-vitamin-a-deficiency-for-public-health.

45 Chang, *Bad Samaritans*, ch. 6; and J. Stiglitz, *Making Globalization Work* (New York: W. W. Norton & Co., 2007), ch. 4.

46 In the end, Harrison was paid only £18,750 (equivalent to about £3 million in today's money). See D. Bradbury, 'Valuing John Harrison's Work – How Much Is That £20,000 Longitude Reward Worth Today?' Office for National Statistics, https://blog.ons.gov.uk/2020/01/17/valuing-john-harrisons-work-how-much-is-that-20000-longitude-reward-worth-today)/. I thank Federico Benninghoff for

reminding of the role of the prize system in the invention of the marine chronometer.

47 In 2021, Uruguay had the highest number of cattle per person at 3. 45 – way ahead of New Zealand in the second place (2.10), which is way ahead of Argentina and Brazil (both at 1.20). The data are from the US Department of Agriculture. See https://beef2live.com/ story-world-cattle-inventory-vs-human-population-country-0-111575

48 S. Meghji, 'How a Uruguayan Town Revolutionised the Way We Eat', *BBC Travel*, 7 January, 2019, https://www.bbc.com/travel/article/ 20190106-how-a-uruguayan-town-revolutionised-the-way-we-eat).

49 See L. Lewowicz, 'Justus von Liebig in Uruguay? His Last Ten Years of Research', paper presented at the 2015 Annual Meeting of the International Society for the Philosophy of Chemistry, https://www. researchgate.net/publication/279263915_Justus_von_Liebig_in_Uru guay_His_last_ten_years_of_research.

50 P. Russell, 'History Cook: Lemco', *Financial Times*, 13 August, 2012, https://www.ft.com/content/6a66606e6-e88a-11e1-8ffc-00144feab49a.

51 Meghji, 'How a Uruguayan Town Revolutionised the Way We Eat'.

52 At its height in November 1942, 9% of all food shipments for Britain were sunk by German naval attacks. L. Collingham, *The Taste of War – World War Two and the Battle for Food* (London: Penguin Books, 2011), pp. 111–13. According to the article 'Uruguayan Town Puts Historic Support to Soviet Troops During Battle of Stalingrad on Display' on the Uruguayan news website MercoPress, 15% of Allied canned meat supply to the Soviet Union also consisted of Uruguayan corned beef. See https://en.mercopress.com/2021/08/09/ uruguayan-town-puts-historic-support-to-soviet-troops-during-battle-of-stalingrad-on-display.

53 P. Pickering and A. Tyrell, *The People's Bread: A History of the Anti-Corn Law League* (London and New York: Leicester University Press, 2000), p. 6.

54 The process leading to the repeal is, like any process leading to a major change, a complex story involving interactions of economic interests, ideas and institutions that this short essay cannot do justice to. For detailed analyses of the 1846 repeal of the Corn Laws, see

Pickering and Tyrell, *The People's Bread;* and S. Schonhardt-Bailey, *From the Corn Laws to Free Trade - Interests, Ideas, and Institutions in Historical Perspective* (Cambridge, Mass.: The MIT Press, 2006). The repeal split the Tory (Conservative) Party, the traditional party of agrarian interests, especially agricultural landlords. After the repeal, those MPs who voted for it, including Robert Peel, the prime minister, left the party and formed a separate political group, known as the Peelites. Due to this split, the Tory Party was out of the government most of the time in the next two decades.

55 M. Friedman and R. Friedman, *Free to Choose* (New York: Harcourt Brace and Jovanovich, 1980), p. 35.

56 Classic examples of this view can be found in J. Bhagwati, *Protectionism* (Cambridge, Mass.: The MIT Press, 1985); and J. Sachs and A. Warner, 'Economic Reform and the Process of Global Integration', *Brookings Papers on Economic Activity*, no. 1 (1995).

57 K. Fielden, 'The Rise and Fall of Free Trade', in C. Bartlett (ed.), *Britain Pre-eminent: Studies in British World Influence in the Nineteenth Century* (London: Macmillan, 1969).

58 P. Bairoch, *Economics and World History – Myths and Paradoxes* (Brighton: Wheatsheaf, 1993), pp. 41–2.

59 Further details can be found in Chang, *Bad Samaritans*, ch. 2. Even more details can be found in Chang, *Kicking Away the Ladder*; and Bairoch, *Economics and World History*.

60 https://www.infoplease.com/world/countries/territories-colonies-and-dependencies.

61 For a chilling report on how the beef industry is destroying the Amazon rainforest to the planet's detriment, see A. Robinson, *Gold, Oil and Avocados: A Recent History of Latin America in Sixteen Commodities* (New York: Melville House Books, 2021), ch. 14, 'Beef (Pará) – The Capital of Ox'.

62 UNCTAD (United Nations Conference on Trade and Development), 'Banana: An INFOCOMM Commodity Profile', 2016, https://unctad.org/system/files/official-document/INFOCOMM_cp01_Banana_en.pdf), p. 5.

63 In 2014, 17 million tons of dessert bananas were exported. Only 0.9 million tons of plantains were. See UNCTAD, 'Banana', p. 5.

64 FAO (Food and Agricultural Organization), 'Banana Facts and Figures', https://www.fao.org/economic/est/est-commodities/oilcrops/banan as/bananafacts#.Ye4JAFjP10s).

65 Ibid.

66 J. Carney and R. Rosomoff, *In the Shadow of Slavery – Africa's Botanical Legacy in the Atlantic World* (Berkeley: University of California Press, 2009), p. 34.

67 Ibid., p. 34.

68 Ibid., p. 34.

69 Ibid., p. 40.

70 Ibid., p. 40.

71 Ibid., p. 35.

72 Robinson, *Gold, Oil and Avocados*, p. 119.

73 G. Livingstone, *America's Backyard: The United States and Latin America from the Monroe Doctrine to the War on Terror* (London: Zed Press, 2009), p. 17.

74 D. Koppel, *The Fate of the Fruit That Changed the World* (New York: Hudson Street Press, 2007), p. 70.

75 Between 1898 and 1934, the US military invaded ten countries in the Caribbean and Latin America no less than twenty-eight times, most of which were on behalf of the banana companies. See Koppel, *The Fate of the Fruit That Changed the World*, p. 63. On further details of the US military invasions and occupations of these countries, see the website of United Fruit Historical Society https://www.unitedfruit. org/chron.htm.

76 Koppel, *Banana: The Fate of the Fruit That Changed the World*, p. 87.

77 E. Posada-Carbo, 'Fiction as History: The *Bananeras* and Gabriel García Márquez's *One Hundred Years of Solitude*', *Journal of Latin American Studies*, vol. 30, no. 2 (1998).

78 On O. Henry's exile in Honduras and the background to the coinage of the term banana republic see M. McLean, 'O. Henry in Honduras', *American Literary Realism, 1870–1910*, vol. 1, no. 3 (Summer 1968). Also see Koppel, *Banana: The Fate of the Fruit That Changed the World*, p. 92.

79 R. Monge-Gonzalez, 'Moving Up the Global Value Chain: The Case of Intel Costa Rica', ILO Americas Technical Report, 2017/8, International

Labour Organization, 2017, https://www.ilo.org/wcmsp5/groups/public/---americas/---ro-lima/documents/publication/wcms_584208.pdf.

80 K. S. Na, 'The Motor Force of Our Economy – 50 Year History of Semi-conductor' (in Korean), http://www.economytalk.kr/news/articleView.html?idxno=130502 (in Korean).

81 https://data.worldbank.org/indicator/TX.VAL.TECH.MF.ZS.

82 For further details, see H.-J. Chang, 'Regulation of Foreign Investment in Historical Perspective', *European Journal of Development Research*, vol. 16, no. 3 (2004).

83 For further details on Ireland, see ibid. On Singapore, see M. Kuan, 'Manufacturing Productive Capabilities: Industrial Policy and Structural Transformation in Singapore', PhD dissertation, University of Cambridge, 2015.

84 T. Standage, *A History of the World in Six Glasses* (New York: Bloomsbury USA, 2006), p. 272.

85 M. Pendergrast, *For God, Country, and Coca-Cola: The Definitive History of the Great American Soft Drink and the Company That Makes It*, 3rd edition (New York: Basic Books, 2013), p. 425.

86 The account of the origin of Coca-Cola, contained in the next three paragraphs, draws mainly on ibid.

87 Standage, *A History of the World in Six Glasses*, p. 250.

88 'History of Coca-Cola', InterExchange, https://www.interexchange.org/articles/career-training-usa/2016/03/08/history-coca-cola/.

89 Pendergrast, *For God, Country, and Coca-Cola*, p. 30.

90 E. Abaka, 'Kola Nut', in Kiple and Ornelas (eds.), *The Cambridge World History of Food*, p. 684.

91 Ibid., pp. 688–90. The quote is from p. 690.

92 D. Starin, 'Kola Nut: So Much More Than Just a Nut', *Journal of the Royal Society of Medicine*, vol. 106, no. 12 (2013).

93 Carney and Rosomoff, *In the Shadow of Slavery – Africa's Botanical Legacy in the Atlantic World* pp. 70–71. Also see Abaka, 'Kola Nut', p. 688.

94 V. Greenwood, 'The Little-known Nut That Gave Coca-Cola Its Name', BBC (https://www.bbc.com/future/article/20160922-the-nut-that-helped-to-build-a-global-empire).

95 Standage, *A History of the World in Six Glasses*, p. 250.

96 B. Delaney, 'It's Not Cocaine: What You Need to Know About the Pope's Coca Drink', *Guardian*, 9 July 2015.

97 See H.-J. Chang, J. Hauge and M. Irfan, *Transformative Industrial Policy for Africa* (Addis Ababa: United Nations Economic Commission for Africa, 2016).

98 According to the UN's Food and Agriculture Organization (FAO), in 2019, Germany produced 3.23 million tonnes of rye, followed by Poland (2.42 million tonnes), Russia (1.43 million tonnes), Denmark (0.88 million) and Belarus (0.75 million tonnes). See http://www.fao.org/faostat/en/#data/QC.

99 In the rich countries, around one-third of taxes are collected in this way, whereas the ratio is over half of government tax revenue in developing countries. See https://www.oecd.org/tax/tax-policy/global-revenue-statistics-database.htm.

100 https://www.ons.gov.uk/peoplepopulationandcommunity/person alandhouseholdfinances/incomeandwealth/bulletins/theeffectsofta xesandbenefitsonhouseholdincome/financialyearending2018.

101 In 2019, the US spent 17% of its GDP on healthcare, against the OECD average of 8.8%. Figures for selected countries are 12% for Switzerland, 11.7% for Germany, 10.3% for the UK, 9.1% for Finland, 8.7% for Italy, 6.8% for Ireland. See https://data.oecd.org/healthres/health-spending.htm.

102 For further discussion of the dynamism-enhancing role of the welfare state, see Chang, *23 Things*, Thing 21, 'Big Government Makes People More Open to Change'.

103 S. Walton, *The Devil's Dinner – A Gastronomic and Cultural History of Chilli Peppers* (New York: St Martin's Press, 2018), p. 21.

104 There are more objective, scientific ways of measuring the hotness of a chilli, such as high-performance liquid chromatography (HPLC), but this method was not invented exclusively for chilli. It is, for example, the technique used in doping tests in sports. See ibid., pp. 18–20.

105 Just flip through any Sichuan cookbook or book about Sichuan food,

in particular the delightful food memoir by the English chef Fuchsia Dunlop, *Sharks Fins and Sichuan Pepper – A Sweet-sour Memoir of Eating in China* (London: Ebury Press, 2011).

106 For a quick introduction to the limits of GDP as a measure of human well-being, see H.-J. Chang, *Economics: The User's Guide* (London: Penguin, 2014). For a more extensive discussion, see D. Pilling, *The Growth Delusion* (London: Bloombsbury, 2018).

107 This involves anticipating needs, identifying options for filling them, making decisions, and monitoring progress. Daminger shows in her study that such cognitive labour, especially anticipation and monitoring, is done disproportionately by women. See A. Daminger, 'The Cognitive Dimension of Household Labor', *American Sociological Review*, vol. 84, no. 4 (2019).

108 See Pilling, *The Growth Delusion*, ch. 3, for different methods of estimating the value of unpaid care work at market prices.

109 See N. Folbre, *The Rise and Decline of Patriarchal Systems – An Intersectional Political Economy* (London: Verso, 2020). For examples of measures to address the gender bias in the pension system, see Women's Budget Group, 'Pensions and Gender Inequality: A Pre-budget Briefing from the Women's Budget Group', March 2020, https://wbg.org.uk/wp-content/uploads/2020/02/final-pensions-2020.pdf.

110 See Folbre, *Rise and Decline*, for a full exposition of how gender discrimination interacts with other practices of discrimination, such as racial discrimination, to 'feminize' certain professions.

111 For further discussions of these changes, see The Care Collective, *The Care Manifesto – The Politics of Interdependence* (London: Verso, 2020).

112 https://www.guinnessworldrecords.com/world-records/largest-empire-by-population.

113 https://www.guinnessworldrecords.com/world-records/largest-empire-(absolute).

114 According to the Office of National Statistics of the United Kingdom, in 1938, the population of Great Britain is estimated to have been 46 million: https://www.ons.gov.uk/peoplepopulationandcommunity/populationandmigration/populationestimates/adhocs/004357g

reatbritainpopulationestimates1937to2014. This means that the population of the empire outside it was 485 million, which is 10.5 times its population.

115 P. K. O'Brien, 'State Formation and the Construction of Institutions for the First Industrial Nation' in H.-J. Chang (ed.), *Institutional Change and Economic Development* (Tokyo: United Nations University Press, and London: Anthem Press, 2007).

116 Ibid.

117 Ibid.

118 P. Laszlo, *Citrus – A History* (Chicago: The University of Chicago Press, 2007), pp. 88–90.

119 C. Price (2017), 'The Age of Scurvy', *Distillations*, Science History Institute, https://www.sciencehistory.org/distillations/the-age-of-scurvy.

120 Ibid.

121 According to the British author Phillip K. Allan, 'Other navies were slow to adopt similar measures. Some, such as the French, were daunted by the cost and logistical challenges involved in supplying such enormous amounts of fruit. Others, with a ready source of lemons, such as Spain, had a prohibition on giving alcohol to their sailors, which made [mixing the juice into grog] unacceptable. Still others viewed the Royal Navy's practice as bizarre.' See P. K. Allan, 'Finding the Cure for Scurvy', *Naval History Magazine*, vol. 35, no. 1 (February 2021), https://www.usni.org/magazines/naval-history-magazine/2021/february/finding-cure-scurvy.

122 The Royal Naval Hospital in Portsmouth treated 1,457 cases of scurvy in 1780. In 1806, it had only two cases of scurvy. See Laszlo, *Citrus*, p. 86.

123 J. Eaglin, 'More Brazilian than Cachaça: Brazilian Sugar-based Ethanol Development in the Twentieth Century', *Latin American Research Review*, vol. 54, no. 4 (2019).

124 Ibid.

125 Strictly speaking, even these alternative energies generate some GHGs, as the construction and the operation of the energy generation facilities involve the use of fossil fuels. For example, the wind turbine is made of steel, resin and cement, while requiring lubricants

during its operation – all of these currently use fossil fuel in their manufacture. On the wind turbine, see V. Smil, 'Why You Need Fossil Fuels to Get Electricity from Wind', in *Numbers Don't Lie: 71 Things You Need to Know About the World* (London: Viking, 2020).

126 For details on how fossil fuels are used in the production of these materials, see V. Smil, *How the World Really Works – A Scientist's Guide to Our Past, Present, and Future* (London: Penguin RandomHouse, 2022).

127 X. Xu et al., 'Global Greenhouse Gas Emissions from Animal-Based Foods Are Twice Those of Plant-based Foods', *Nature Food*, September 2021.

128 Ibid.

129 For further details, see A. Anzolin and A. Lebdioui, 'Three Dimensions of Green Industrial Policy in the Context of Climate Change and Sustainable Development', *European Journal of Development Research*, vol. 33, no. 2 (2021).

130 This is in line with the fundamental insight of the Behaviouralist School of economics, which says that the most important constraint to decision-making is our limited mental capacity (what the School calls 'bounded rationality') rather than lack of information. On this (and other) school(s) of economics, see chapter 4 of my book *Economics: The User's Guide*.

131 In sailing the Indian and the Pacific Oceans, the Europeans had to hire Arab and South Asian seamen, who knew those oceans much better than they did – see J. Hobson, *The Eastern Origins of Western Civilization* (Cambridge: Cambridge University Press, 2004), pp. 140–44. These seamen were called *lascars* and included the ancestors of the Sylheti 'Indian' restaurateurs of Britain today, featured in Spices.

132 For some policy proposals, see Chang, *23 Things*, Thing 22, 'Financial markets need to become less, not more, efficient'; and Chang, *Economics: The User's Guide*, ch. 8, 'Trouble at the Fidelity Fiduciary Bank'.

133 On the controversy about jelly in trifle, see 'No Such Thing as a Mere Trifle' in WordofMouth Blog, https://www.theguardian.com/lifeandstyle/wordofmouth/poll/2009/dec/21/perfect-trifle-jelly.

134 B. Neuburger, 'California's Migrant Farmworkers: A Caste System Enforced by State Power', *Monthly Review*, vol. 71, no. 1 (2019). Mexican farm workers are important not just in California. According to Neuburger, around 80% of US farm workers are immigrants, with the majority being from Mexico.

135 E. Schlosser, 'In the Strawberry Fields', *The Atlantic*, November 1995, https://www.theatlantic.com/magazine/archive/1995/11/in-the-strawberry-fields/305754/.

136 Ibid.

137 Since most farmworkers are employed on a seasonal basis rather than throughout the year, annual incomes can often be far below that suggested by their hourly wages. The Economic Policy Institute, a Washington, D.C.-based progressive think-thank, estimates that, in 2015, the average farmworker earned an annual income of $17,500, less than 60% of the full-time equivalent calculated from hourly wages ($12–14, which is higher than the minimum wage in California, which was $10–10.50 in 2017). See P. Martin and D. Costa, 'Farmworker Wages in California: Large Gaps between Full-time Equivalent and Actual Earnings', 2017, https://www.epi.org/blog/farmworker-wages-in-california-large-gap-between-full-time-equivalent-and-actual-earnings/.

138 K. Hodge, 'Coronavirus Accelerates the Rise of the Robot Harvester', *Financial Times*, 1 July 2020, https://www.ft.com/content/eaaf12e8–907a-11ea-bc44-dbf6756c871a.

139 J. Bessen , *Learning by Doing – The Real Connection between Innovation, Wages, and Wealth* (New Haven: Yale University Press, 2015), pp. 96–7. If we consider that the US population grew by six times during this period (from 12.8 million to 76.2 million), which Bessen does not, this represents an increase of 66.7% on a per capita basis.

140 Further details on how the ALMP works in Sweden and Finland can be found in D. Stuckler and S. Basu, *The Body Economic – Why Austerity Kills* (New York: Basic Books, 2013), ch. 7, 'Returning to Work'.

141 E. Purser, 'The Great Transatlantic Chocolate Divide', *BBC News Magazine*, 15 December 2009 (http://news.bbc.co.uk/1/hi/magazine/8414488.

stm#:~:text=A%20Cadbury%20Dairy%20Milk%20bar,Hershey%20
bar%20contains%20just%2011%25).

142 According to the latest available data from the UNIDO (United
Nations Industrial Development Organization), in 2015, Switzerland
produced MVA (manufacturing value-added) per capita of $14,404 (in
2010 prices) per person, by far the highest in the world. The second
highest, by some margin, was Singapore, at $9,537. The corresponding
figures were $9,430 for Germany (ranked no. 3), $5,174 for the US and
$2,048 for China. See https://www.unido.org/sites/default/files/
files/2017-11/IDR2018_FULL%20REPORT.pdf.

143 See Chang, *Economics: The User's Guide*, pp. 264–5.

Index